# NOODLES EVERY DAY

# NOODLES
# EVERY DAY

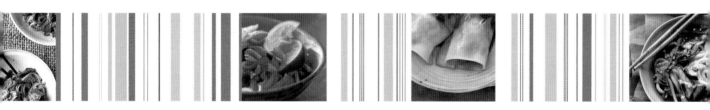

*by* CORINNE TRANG
*Photographs by* MAURA McEVOY

DELICIOUS ASIAN RECIPES
FROM RAMEN TO RICE STICKS

CHRONICLE BOOKS
SAN FRANCISCO

Library of Congress Cataloging-in-Publication Data available.

ISBN 978-0-8118-6143-4

Manufactured in China.

Designed and typeset by McGuire Barber Design
Food styling by Frank Mentesana
Prop styling by Christine Rudolph

10 9 8 7 6 5 4 3 2 1

Chronicle Books LLC
680 Second Street
San Francisco, California 94107

www.chroniclebooks.com

To my daughter, Colette Trang McDonough:

You have reconnected me to the simple pleasures of noodles.

# ACKNOWLEDGMENTS

This book would not have been possible without the encouragement and support of my husband, Michael McDonough. After many years, he remains my greatest fan, never too tired to lend a helping hand, or if too tired, never complaining about it. And after his too-numerous-to-count noodle tastings, he always managed a smile and enthusiasm for more. Thank you, darling.

Recipe tastings would not have been possible without my dedicated assistant and recipe tester Graciel Caces, who always came eager to test and learn. Thank you for being so enthusiastic and gracious.

I am ever so grateful to my literary agent, Angela Miller, for continuing to support my work; to Bill LeBlond at Chronicle for encouraging me to write and turn the complex and vast subject of Asian noodles into the simple, accessible recipes listed here; to Amy Treadwell for being so diligent; and to Deborah Kops for her excellent copyediting. I thank you all for keeping me focused.

To designer Patrick Barber, food photographer Maura McEvoy, food stylist Frank Mentesana, and prop stylist Christine Rudolph, for translating the recipes into beautiful pages, I also say thank you. You have added texture, color, and shape to my words. Thank you for having the vision.

To Beth Shepard, for engaging me in multiple platforms to promote what I love. You are remarkable. Thank you for your clarity and know-how.

To Maite Goff and Lisa Coker at Panos brands, for providing me with the all-natural line of KA-ME Asian noodles and condiments in time for testing the recipes. Your product made it so easy to re-create authentic, classic, and contemporary Asian noodle meals. Thank you for participating so generously.

To my friends and family who continue to be supportive and understanding when I don't show up for events or gatherings. My heart always says "yes," the scheduling pressures often dictate differently. Thank you for yesterday, today, and tomorrow. For this will likely not be the last time I say "yes," "maybe," and "no" simultaneously.

And with that, I raise a glass to you all!

CT

# CONTENTS

# INTRODUCTION

Noodle dishes are eaten as full meals, light meals, and snacks throughout Asia at all hours of the day and night, serving as a kind of sophisticated fast food. My brothers and I grew up eating these noodle dishes in family homes in France and Southeast Asia. When traveling for research, I have enjoyed freshly made *mee krob* (sweet and crispy fried rice vermicelli) and pad Thai (page 125) from open-air food carts at the midnight bazaar of Chiang Mai, Thailand. And I've had a simple breakfast of chicken, egg, dark soy sauce, and pungent spices with fried egg noodles called *mi goreng* as breakfast at a Balinese bed-and-breakfast in Ubud while on vacation. My four-year-old daughter always looks forward to the black soba noodles with tofu and vegetables we share at our local Japanese restaurant in New York City. And my husband will do handstands for a special fresh wide rice noodle and shrimp dish I make for Sunday brunch (page 161). My family and I have come to love the food that Asia has raised to a virtual culinary art form, the humble noodle. I have experienced it in its many guises—from a simple soba noodle with a bit of soy sauce and sesame oil dipping sauce on the side to the complex and fragrant flavorings of rice noodles with vegetables, pork, coconut, and curry seasoning, known as Singapore Noodles (page 117).

Almost everyone has had a plate of wheat noodle–based chow mein. At restaurants, you and your family may have also experienced more sophisticated dishes, such as Chinese cold sesame noodles; wontons in broth; stir-fried egg noodles with beef and broccoli; the Vietnamese rice noodle soup known as *pho*; stir-fried broad rice noodles with beef, scallion, and bean sprouts; Korean stir-fried cellophane noodles, known as *chap chae*; or Japanese soba. It must be noted that pad Thai—the stir-fried Thai noodle dish made with rice noodles, eggs, fish sauce, tamarind, bean sprouts,

peanuts, and a variety of proteins—ranks among Americans' favorite international dishes. In fact, McDonald's was reportedly considering adding Thai dishes to its U.S. menus in 2006. That same year, the *New York Times* suggested pad Thai as an appropriate snack to be made by moms and kids (see "Generation Pad Thai" by Jennifer Steinhauer in the *New York Times*, January 15, 2006).

In *Noodles Every Day: Delicious Asian Recipes from Ramen to Rice Sticks*, I combine family favorites that I have enjoyed from the time I was a child, familiar restaurant dishes, and interpretations of dishes that I have learned while traveling as an adult in China, Japan, Korea, the Philippines, Indonesia, Vietnam, Cambodia, and Thailand. All of these have been adapted for the contemporary Western kitchen. Noodles form the basis for innumerable Asian dishes, and even a passing acquaintance with a few recipes will open a world of new culinary experiences for most cooks.

Here I explore the idea that these small Asian snack dishes can be the foundations for quick, healthful, and wondrously varied meals, which can be prepared by any home cook. Most include only a few ingredients, go from package and cutting board to skillet and table in about 30 minutes or less, and require no special skills or foreknowledge of Asian cooking to prepare. They can be enjoyed by dyed-in-the-wool meat eaters, vegetarians of all stripes, and serious vegans—depending on the recipe selected and how the ingredients are parsed out. Almost everything you need to succeed in creating great recipes and bold flavors can be found in the international foods aisle of your local supermarket. And the recipes in this book will allow you to extend your range once you master the basics. In essence, if you can make spaghetti, you can cook these dishes.

My hope, then, is to wrestle the extraordinary diversity of Asian noodles into a few categories, and to proceed with a sense of adventure and invention. Broadly speaking, you can group Asian noodles into dry and fresh types, and break them down by main ingredient from there. Surprisingly, perhaps, you won't need any extensive understanding of country of origin because most of these noodles are used all throughout Asia. When it makes sense, I give the name of the Italian pasta that is roughly equivalent as a sort of shorthand. When an item is unusual or especially suited to a dish, I do identify it as such. And I give the traditional names of specific dishes and note their roots when appropriate.

A balance of ingredient types, with an eye toward healthy eating, is discernable in all the recipes here. They are relatively low in calories without sacrificing flavor. Among the heartier dishes, there are always enough vegetables to balance the protein, and enough carbohydrates to provide quick energy without dominating the dish. Sauces are conceived to complement the basic noodle—more like the Northern Italian notion of "staining" the pasta with sauce than the Southern Italian tradition of a thick tomato-and-meat ragu.

## SOME NOODLE HISTORY (BUT NOT TOO MUCH)

While this book is in no way intended as a dissertation on Asian noodles, the history of noodles is useful as a backstory when cooking, and I find that it makes for interesting conversation at the table. I should note that I generally prefer to steer clear of the "origin of noodles" question, not because it isn't fun (it is), but because it can become a bit of a quagmire in professional circles if it isn't handled deftly. Food history is serious stuff and archeology is often involved. Academic reputations can rise and fall based on a page in a cookbook or an ingredient discovered out of context.

On an informal and nonprofessional level, however, I like to give a nod to my Chinese father's long-standing and often passionately expressed assertion that noodles started among the Chinese, and not among the other two contenders—the Italians and Arabs. At least one version of modern conventional wisdom holds that Chinese noodles were invented elsewhere, derived from similar foods developed in southwest and central Asia about two thousand years ago. The great Arab civilizations, the theory goes, first invented and then shared noodle-making techniques with the Romans. The Romans, it continues, popularized them and brought them to greater Italy, and eventually to China via Marco Polo and other trade-route adventurers. Other variations on this theme exist, but you get the idea: in essence, the Chinese received the noodle; they didn't invent it. "Nonsense!" my father would respond in annoyance upon hearing this argument.

In 2005 the plot thickened, however. That year the whole noodle-origin debate was stood on its head by a discovery made in Lajia, the so-called Pompeii of China. There, at an archeology site on the Yellow River southwest of Beijing, a vessel of millet noodles was unearthed. Radiocarbon dating indicated the noodles were four-thousand-year-old, late-Neolithic period foodstuff—caveman stuff, essentially. Given that millet had been cultivated for three thousand years *prior to* the time that now-storied vessel was originally filled with slender strands, my father has a big grin on his face whenever the subject comes up.

"Everything started in China," my father likes to say. "Nothing is harder to nail down than a noodle's origin," says my husband, smiling. We won't settle it here.

## ASIAN NOODLE TYPES

Asian noodles can be handily subdivided into five basic categories: wheat (udon and somen), egg (*lo mien* and ramen), buckwheat (soba), rice noodles (*banh trang*), and cellophane (mung bean– or sweet potato–based). Then there are the variations: Rice flour–based dough includes wide flat rice papers for spring and summer rolls. Wheat and egg doughs are similarly employed for wontons and hundreds of different dumplings. I also think of buns as a variation of a noodle because they are considered snacks in much the same way as noodle dishes.

Asian noodles may be purchased fresh or dried. The "fresh" category includes precooked noodles. In addition, noodles come in a variety of shapes: short and long, thin and thick, and curly and flat. Some are cut, while others are rolled or pulled. To complicate matters further, there are hundreds of regional variations. The preparation techniques for all of these noodles include boiling, stir-frying, steaming, soaking, deep-frying, and braising. And the types of vegetable and protein combinations are as numerous as the ingredients themselves. In short, Asia is a treasure trove of noodle types and related recipes.

This reality can seem daunting to the uninitiated Westerner. I particularly remember my husband's first encounter with what he called "the giant noodle wall" in a Vietnamese shop in New York's Chinatown. He is an adventurous eater with an endless passion for culinary knowledge, but this "first encounter of the noodle kind," as he described it, was a bit too much, even for him. Eventually, he says, guided by my tutelage and a considerable number of meals, the wall seemed to break down into categories and types so that he can now differentiate among the white, clear, brown, green, mottled, speckled, fresh, dried, and frozen varieties without too much consternation. (This is also where that little bit of history comes in handy: the wheat noodles come from the north, and rice and egg noodles from the south. Now you're off and running.)

Remember that the type of noodle you are working with— wheat, egg, buckwheat, rice, or cellophane—is as important as the country of origin, if not more so. Most Asian noodles originated in China. That's why a Japanese noodle can be used in a Chinese stir-fry with little consequence except a full tummy and a smile. And that is why, for the most part, I can buy similar noodles from a Vietnamese shop, a Japanese grocery store, and a Chinese street cart.

Noodle cooking is a large, highly developed, and distinct part of Asian cuisine. It is a major preparation technique for hundreds of dishes. Like rice, noodles are not just ingredients. They are the underpinnings of one of the world's oldest food cultures and a window onto understanding it.

## NOODLE TYPES

Rice noodles are a sort of Asian culinary workhorse. They are certainly the most straightforward of all. The dough is never flavored or blended with other ingredients. Having originated in the rice-growing southern regions of China, they are now available throughout Asia and the West in numerous shapes and sizes. Wheat and wheat-based varieties originated in the northern wheat-based agricultural areas of China, and now are also available in many parts of the world. They include plain wheat noodles (such as the Japanese udon noodles you find in soups), wheat and egg noodles (similar in color to Italian semolina-based pasta or German egg noodles), and a hearty variety that combines wheat flour and buckwheat (also known as soba, and often found in Japanese restaurant dishes in the West).

Wheat-based noodles are versatile. The dough may be lightly flavored with crab, shrimp, or vegetables. Buckwheat is sometimes infused with green tea, yielding a noodle that is green in color and that remembers the slightly bitter note of the powdered green tea that was added to the dough. Cellophane noodles (also known as glass noodles), which are made from mung bean starch or sweet potato starch, are also readily available. They are chewy in texture and valued because they are virtually flavorless, allowing them to play humble host to a variety of other ingredients and flavors, usually in stir-fries, stews, and soups. All noodle types are widely available in Asian and Western markets. They are also readily available by mail-order or on the Internet. (See the Mail-Order Sources on page 162.)

Sorghum noodles and millet noodles (the descendants of the the above-mentioned Neolithic noodles) are eaten principally in China's northern provinces. These whole-grain noodles, which are similar to buckwheat, are often treated as specialty items and can be hard to find. I only mention them here so that you may remember to ask for them the next time you go eat at an authentic Chinese restaurant. They are definitely worth a try.

It is important to note, however, that with a few exceptions, Asian noodles are often used interchangeably. This differentiates them from Italian pastas, many of which are designed for use in a series of specific dishes (think lasagna, for example). The Chinese cook looking for hearty sorghum will just as readily grab wheat or egg noodles, if that is all that is available. I use Japanese buckwheat noodles in Chinese-style stir-fried noodle dishes when the winter winds are blowing and I crave a filling dish without piling on the meat, for example.

Now, in deference to my husband's "giant noodle wall" experience, I have to admit that shopping for Asian noodles is sometimes overwhelming. But they are just little strips of dough and although there are exceptions, they are all basically interchangeable. Bear in mind that like many Italian pastas, a thicker, more filling noodle will hold up to hearty meat dishes, while a lighter, thinner variety might do well with an array of spring vegetables. You could, I suppose, take the path of the purist in these matters, heeding some sense that each noodle has a place in its own special dish. Purists take note, however: In many Asian restaurants, the guest is asked to select his or her preferred noodle type in a given dish, and some menus list the various noodle varieties to simplify ordering. "Would you like soba or udon noodles?" asks the waitperson. "Oh, egg noodles? Okay!" More often than not in Asian restaurant kitchens, a noodle dish is made as you wish, and that is certainly the case in home kitchens.

Let me bolster your confidence a bit more: Asian noodles often cook in 5 minutes or less (and sometimes in just a few seconds), irrespective of whether the noodle is fresh or dry. And if you can't find fresh Asian noodles, dried versions of many Asian noodles are available as substitutes. Finally, noodles are eaten variously as snacks and side dishes, as main dishes and in soups. They appear in braised and stir-fried dishes; sauced and dry; with meat, fish, shellfish, poultry, and game; with vegetables and starch tubers; and as an accompaniment to rice. In sum, noodles are arguably the original Asian fast food, and one of the most versatile foodstuffs on earth.

## DUMPLINGS AND BUNS

A cookbook on Asian noodles would not be complete without a chapter on dumplings and buns. Considered to be part of the same food group as noodles, these have a place in my childhood memories of wonderful food. Quite frankly, I'm hooked on dumplings. The Chinese say "*chi fan pao,*" meaning "70 percent full," and this is exactly when you should leave the table. Show me a dumpling, and that rule goes out the window, however. My favorite among favorites is the classic wonton filled with pork and shrimp (page 147), but Pork and Watercress Dumplings (page 150) are right up there, too. Served with an accompanying sauce (which is often meant to balance and lift a dumpling's flavor), these little gems can be a divine snack or light meal. Buns stuffed with flavored pork (page 148) or chicken are also associated culturally with traditional noodle foods, though the connection may not be obvious at first. Barbecued pork buns, for example, are steamed or baked until golden. They come small or large, and are often eaten with dumplings or by themselves as a snack.

The best, most coherent, and time-honored noodle, dumpling, and bun experience is *dim sum*, which means, roughly translated, "touch of the heart." These are essentially small—sometimes bite-size—items that are fried or steamed and are most often served from little wheeled carts, where they are kept hot. Dim sum includes savory dishes based on meat, seafood, and vegetables, as well as sweet desserts and fruit. They are usually served in the same bamboo or small metal steamer basket in which they were cooked (generally three at a time). The meal is ritualized and drawn out (to encourage nibbling and conversation). Tea is the traditional accompaniment.

## A BIT OF PERSONAL NOODLE HISTORY

My personal history includes a good amount of noodle making, prepping, cooking, and—I confess—slurping (it's polite at Asian tables). Because my Chinese father worked in the food industry in Lower Manhattan's Chinatown, he knew all of the best Asian restaurants in the city and what dishes to order where. One of his cardinal rules was that each restaurant, no matter how modest, would have one or

two brilliant dishes that stood head and shoulders above everything else on the menu. The trick, in his estimation, was to know exactly where to go for what.

Our favorite wonton place was a good example. It never failed to deliver the best wontons we had eaten anywhere, easily trumping more expensive versions in much tonier (and roomier) restaurants.

This small noodle shop in Chinatown was about 200 square feet, and always crammed with patrons. It had a wonderful silver sign outside that was prominent enough to be seen from a block or so away. The cook worked in the window—not for show but for lack of space (though the show was definitely enticing). We would place our order in one Chinese dialect, and then hear it shouted across the room at the cook in another. Soon delicate, bite-size dumplings of egg or wheat wrappers, folded to encase ground pork and shrimp, and set afloat in a fragrant gingery chicken broth, would arrive. I sometimes added a dash or two of dark sesame oil and pungent, freshly sliced scallions.

The family also sometimes ventured out of Chinatown, and up into Midtown Manhattan's Koreatown, not far from Herald Square and Macy's block-long flagship department store. We would always go with a group of relatives or friends so that we could order a wide array of dishes. Spicy preserved vegetable kimchi would be set out for us as soon as we sat down. Then we ordered family-style. *Chap chae* (page 137), a mixture of sliced beef and vegetables, seasoned with soy sauce, sesame oil, and spices, and stir-fried with sweet potato starch noodles, was a must. Slippery and chewy in texture, these cellophane noodles turned transparent when cooked and were light in flavor—light enough to take on the flavor of other ingredients beautifully.

Much later in life, in Chiang Mai, Thailand, I enjoyed the *mee krob* and pad Thai mentioned above and also *kao soi* (page 118), a rice noodle curry soup with chicken, pork, or shrimp, fragrant with lime juice, lemongrass, kaffir lime leaves, and coconut milk. In Hanoi, or down south in Ho Chi Minh City (formerly known as Saigon), I've had my fill of the family favorite, *pho* (page 121). In Vietnam, you can eat *pho* in the noodle shops, or on the sidewalk where it is prepared by street hawkers.

I have also enjoyed the experience of fresh buckwheat noodles in the Japanese ritualized dish called *zaru soba* (page 98). These soba are loaded with distinct earthy and nutty flavors that no other noodle has. My meal was prepared as reverential "dinnertime theater" by a noodle master who dressed the part and performed his magic in a special glass kiosk set in the middle of a New York City Japanese restaurant. Watching the noodle master create his specialty right before my eyes was truly compelling and delicious. The master took great, almost meditative, pleasure in the process of making the dough, mixing buckwheat flour and regular wheat flour and then introducing spring water into the well he created in the center of the combined flours. He slowly worked the basic ingredients into a dough with a good amount of elasticity. Rolling it out with a long dowel, he formed it into a thin rectangle, then floured and folded it into multiple layers.

The noodle master then sliced through the layers with a large metal knife specifically designed for this soba. The resulting thin strands were then tossed in more flour, shaken, shaped into single portions, and set in a wooden box with a mesh bottom. These fresh noodles were light beige and grainy, unlike the smooth, dark-brown dried soba available in stores. They were boiled for a few seconds,

chilled in iced spring water, and served on a bamboo mat set in a beautiful, square red lacquered box for collecting any drained water. Robust and nutty, the soba was garnished with *nori* and served with a soy-based dipping sauce on the side. The dish was ultimately simplicity itself, allowing the lucky diner to focus on the flavor of the noodle. The experience was ethereal.

## NOODLE PLEASURES

Soups based on noodles loom large on my favorites list. Consider *pho* (page 121): Rice noodles (fresh or dried) are precooked in boiling water, then added to a broth made from meaty beef bones, onion, cinnamon, star anise, and cloves. The result is an amazingly subtle concoction that defies easy description but definitely yields fragrant aromas and all the layered flavor notes that went into the soup.

Then the fun begins: you get to add various ingredients to your personal bowl. First, you cook super-thin raw beef in the steaming broth. Then come freshly torn herbs, such as cilantro, saw leaf, and Thai basil; crunchy bean sprouts; tangy lemon or lime wedges; and sliced hot chilies, each to your liking. Finally there's sweet hoisin sauce, salty fish sauce, or hot and spicy (or garlicky) chili sauce. My mother, a wonderful French cook, learned the secrets of *pho* from her Asian mother- and sisters-in-law. It was served all year round, whether it was zero or one hundred degrees Farenheit outside. The dish would either warm us up or make us sweat, but it was always welcome. And we always had seconds.

Another one of my favorite rice noodle soups—one that I am delighted to share here—is made with ground pork and dried or fresh shrimp, fried garlic in oil, cilantro, and sliced red Thai chilies (page 113). The broth, made with preserved daikon and dried squid, is sweet, smoky, and salty at the same time. The dish can be served with the noodles in it or as a "dry soup," with the noodles and other ingredients in a bowl and the broth on the side, as noodle soups are often served in Vietnam and Cambodia. In the all-in-one-bowl version, the broth keeps the noodles hot. In the separate-but-equal version, the broth is sipped as a palate cleanser after each slurp of noodles. Either way is authentic, delicious, and works just fine.

A favorite egg noodle dish is stir-fried sliced tender beef and crunchy Chinese broccoli (page 82). Here thick egg noodles take on the combined flavors of the sirloin marinated in soy and sesame oil and the sweet leafy greens. I reserve these slightly chewy noodles for winter, when I want a little extra oomph in the bowl. Another great egg noodle dish included here is made with thin, somewhat curly noodles, which are like a fresh version of dried Japanese ramen noodles. The curlicues are set afloat in a smoky broth made with sliced five-spice-seasoned roast duck. This is perfect for a light dinner in front of the fireplace. The same noodles are equally delicious when combined with pork and shrimp wontons and served in a light chicken broth (page 77).

My little daughter, Colette, calls her cellophane noodles "magic noodles" because they start out opaque and become transparent and glassy when cooked. These noodles are traditionally used in the classic Korean *chap chae* (page 137). This single-skillet or wok dish contains shredded beef and vegetables such as carrots, cabbage, and shiitakes. A variation, the humble, home-style Chinese version of the dish, is braised in a clay pot. A snap to make, the cellophane noodles are cooked in chicken stock with dried shrimp, dried shiitakes, ginger, scallion, soy sauce, and sesame oil (page 141). They retain a pleasant, chewy texture while absorbing the combined earthy and nutty flavors of the other ingredients. Shredded chicken can be added to the dish for a heartier meal. If you want to get into clay-pot cooking, this is the perfect one-step meal to start with.

My family enjoys a wonderfully humble soba-based dish in a fun little Japanese restaurant close to our home in New York City. Stir-fried soba, or *yaki soba*, is a dish generally made with egg noodles. I like to drive the chef crazy and ask him to make it with buckwheat noodles. Though not strictly traditional, it is absolutely delicious, hearty, and healthful when broccoli florets, red onions, carrots, and chicken are added to the mix (page 101).

## ABOUT THE ORGANIZATION OF THIS BOOK

Organized around a pantry of easily found ingredients, this book is for the noodle enthusiast who wants to explore the flavors of Asia and for the serious Asian cook. As in my previous book, *The Asian Grill: Great Recipes, Bold Flavors*, the recipes are easy to prepare and emphasize authentic Asian flavors. I also mention the Asian specialty markets that carry unusual, seasonal, or regional items when appropriate or absolutely necessary for a special dish.

A chapter is devoted to each of the five types of noodles— wheat, egg, buckwheat, rice, and cellophane. A sixth chapter focuses on dumplings and related foods. You'll also find chapters describing essential ingredients, cooking equipment and techniques, and basic Asian condiments and their preparation—all helpful in getting started. And in the note accompanying each recipe, I always describe the dish, discuss the traditional ingredients, and suggest substitutions when appropriate. Whenever I can I set the scene with a story, a bit of history, or an anecdote, sharing the pleasure of the kitchen as best I can. This is how I learned to cook with my Asian family and my French mother: aware of the evolution of any dish, but relaxed and confident of being able to explore and create.

# BASIC ASIAN INGREDIENTS

CHAPTER

Guided by the rich traditions of classic Asian cooking, I have created recipes for this book that are quick, simple, healthful, and varied in flavor. Remarkably, all this can be achieved with relatively few basic ingredients, all of which are listed below.

Of course, I had a lot of help. I used to hear from students and friends that Asian cooking seemed intimidating because it involved so many ingredients that were daunting, complicated, and unfamiliar, or—my favorite turn of phrase—mystery ingredients. That may have been true about twenty years ago, when most Asian ingredients were available only in Asian markets, and the thought of venturing off to Chinatown was overwhelming. But attitudes have changed, ingredients are easier to find, and the refrain of "daunting, complicated, and unfamiliar" has been replaced to a large extent by "exciting."

These days people are more excited about preparing Asian food for a number of reasons: the economic opening of Asia to the West, the rapid development of its great coastal cities and inland manufacturing cities, the availability of direct flights to Asia, and the growth of Asian food tours, a wonderful development. In addition, the influx of Asian immigrants to North America and the appearance of their native ingredients in supermarket aisles have helped Asian foods become more accessible and commonplace. As a result, Americans have become more adventuresome diners. I am often reminded of this, especially when I travel to Asia and see Western tourists eating their way through each village, town, or city, trying all sorts of foods, and exploring new textures and flavors. No longer curious onlookers, these seasoned gourmets want the foods they encountered abroad upon returning home.

Ironically, while we are enjoying our broadening experiences more, we have less time for them. So while I am pleased to share my understanding of an ingredient, I also realize that you have limited time and energy during your busy day. No matter—traditional Asian culture values efficiency. Many of the dishes here are of the type and style that would be found in home kitchens, workplaces, and informal get-togethers at all times of the day or night. And the ingredients are as accessible and as easy to handle as cooking oil and salt are in Western recipes. Your supermarket probably carries the few Asian ingredients needed to create the authentic noodle recipes that follow.

First, a few notes on storage, shelf life, dry and fresh ingredients, and other Asian basics.

## STORING ASIAN INGREDIENTS (AND KNOWING WHEN TO THROW THEM OUT)

### Storing Sauces

Be sure to refrigerate sauces such as hoisin sauce, chili-garlic sauce, and other wet condiments after they have been opened. This will ensure freshness and extend the life of your condiments by a couple of months.

Soy sauce (from China, Korea, and Japan) and fish sauce (from Vietnam, Thailand, and the Philippines) are considered the salts of Asia. But they offer more than a salty character to a dish. Like all Asian ingredients, these seasonings are used as an overall strategy to create balance and harmony in a meal, including many of the noodle recipes in this book.

Soy sauce and fish sauce do not last forever, however. Old sauces may not kill you (they are probably okay to eat), but once opened, they are at their best for about 9 months. When kept longer, they become stale and lose the delicate flavor they normally impart to foods. Refrigerating these sauces will extend their useful life by another 2 to 3 months—in other words, for up to 1 year. My 1-year rule for condiments is easy to remember. If you've had a sauce for some time but are unsure exactly how long, remember that it is so inexpensive that it isn't worth thinking about. Just toss it and buy a new bottle.

One useful trick is to write the purchase date on the label as a reminder. (In fact, it is a good idea to do this with all wet and dried ingredients.) And finally, condiments like soy sauce and fish sauce come in different sizes. Buy according to what you think you will use up within 6 months to a year so as to eliminate any waste. But if you go through fish sauce, soy sauce, or any other wet condiment as quickly I do (within 1 to 6 months), keeping track of the date will not be an issue.

## Buying and Storing Dried Spices

When selecting dried spices, be sure they are bright in color. Just because herbs and spices are dried does not mean they should look dull. On the contrary, they should be beautiful and vibrant. For example, if red pepper flakes look dull or mint is a dark grayish-green, it has probably been sitting on the shelf far too long. Look for vibrant red pepper flakes or powders and bright green mint. While the shade of a curry powder may depend on the ratio of the spices in the mix, it, too, should look bright, rather than dull.

My 1-year rule applies to herbs and spices as well as condiments. They should not be kept any longer than that, so be sure to buy them in small quantities and purchase only as much as you think you will use within a year. Remember, the dried spices you buy are weeks if not months old by the time you get them. Shipped in bulk to a supplier, they are then packaged and possibly repackaged for distribution. Somewhere in this equation, the spices have been ware-

housed more than once before they get to the market. Once there, some herbs and spices will hit the shelves immediately, while others will be stored yet again until some shelf space frees up, which may take days, weeks, or months, depending on how fast the merchandise moves. Once on the shelf they are subject to bright, powerful store lighting, which is not recommended for spices, especially those sold in bulk, or packaged in either clear glass or plastic containers or bags.

Buy from a good source and store them in a dark, cool place to preserve them. For oily spices such as cumin, caraway, and other seeds, watch out for a telltale rancid taste. Discard any item that is even slightly rancid.

## Storing Oil and Vinegar

Oils should be changed every 3 to 6 months because once the container is opened, they start losing freshness and flavor and start turning rancid. Keep oils in a dark, cool place, such as a cool pantry or the refrigerator, making sure to tighten the screw top. Some oils, such as dark sesame oil, solidify in the refrigerator, while others do not. If the oil solidifies, it will return to its liquid state at room temperature, so no worries.

Vinegars should also be kept in a dark, cool place, though not necessarily the refrigerator. Be sure to tighten the screw top so as not to allow any evaporation, which starts as soon as the bottle is opened.

## Buying and Storing Fresh Ingredients

The fresh ingredients you will need most for the recipes in this book are garlic, shallots, scallions, ginger, cilantro, lemongrass, Thai basil, lime, lemon, and Thai chilies. The garlic, shallots, limes, and lemons can be kept in a dark, cool place. Store scallions, lemongrass, chilies, and leafy green herbs in the refrigerator.

Fresh ginger can also be refrigerated for a few days without any special care. To extend its life, put it in a bowl, and cover it with water. Put the bowl in the refrigerator and change the water daily. This will keep the ginger fresh for an extra week or so.

The most exotic vegetables you will need are bok choy, edible chrysanthemum leaves, Chinese broccoli, and watercress. If you cannot find any of these, replace them with other leafy greens, such as spinach or romaine lettuce.

To keep any leafy greens fresh for at least a week, wash them and dry them thoroughly with a salad spinner. Transfer the greens to a large plastic bag and seal, without squeezing out too much of the air. The leaves should not be too crowded in the bag.

## THE BASIC ASIAN PANTRY

A basic Asian pantry will include sugar, salt, black or white pepper, thin soy sauce, rice vinegar, rice wine (for example, sake), dried red chilies, curry powder, cornstarch (or tapioca starch), dark sesame oil, and a high-temperature cooking oil, such as peanut oil. In addition to these, be sure to have a supply of fresh ginger, garlic, and scallions (also known as green onions or bunching onions). These few ingredients are what many Asian households have on hand at all times, and are as common in Asian cooking as your salt, pepper, and Italian seasonings, for example.

If you feel confident and adventurous, you can also stock up on fish sauce, mirin (a light syrup made with rice wine), hoisin sauce, chili-garlic sauce (smooth or chunky), five-spice powder, rice flour, Thai curry paste, coconut milk, and fresh lemongrass, cilantro, and mint. These are a bit beyond basic, but still very easily found, if not at your local market, then certainly in a health food store.

### Asian Noodles

Each of the five chapters on noodles has a detailed introduction to the type of noodle it covers—wheat, egg, buckwheat, rice, or cellophane (made from mung bean or sweet potato starch). The sixth chapter introduces you to the wheat- or egg-based wrappers for making dumplings, the egg- or rice-based wrappers for spring rolls, and the yeasty dough for making buns. For this reason, I have omitted detailed descriptions of noodles in this chapter. I encourage you to read each introduction in Chapters 4 through 9.

Store fresh Asian noodles in the refrigerator, where they will keep for up to 2 days. Dried noodles should be stored in a dark, cool place. Dried wheat, buckwheat, and egg noodles will keep for up to 6 months, while dried rice noodles and cellophane noodles will keep for 1 year before they go stale.

Fresh or fresh-frozen Japanese udon (a thick wheat noodle) and fresh buckwheat noodles can be found in Japanese or Korean markets. Fresh egg, wheat, and rice noodles will be the most difficult to come by. You will need to make a trip to Chinatown, if you live near one. Some Asian markets will sometimes special-order them as well. For most of the recipes that call for fresh noodles, however, rest assured that their dried noodle counterparts will work as well. In a pinch, fresh Italian pasta such as capellini (angel hair), spaghetti, or linguine can be used in egg noodle recipes. However, the texture will be a bit different and the flavor will be much less egg-y than that of their Chinese or Asian cousins.

Dried Asian noodles are easy to find, especially ramen (Japanese egg noodles), rice noodles, udon, somen (Japanese thin round wheat noodles), and cellophane noodles. These are available in the international section of your local supermarket. While you may not find as wide a variety of these there as you would in Asian markets, the ones that you do find will give you more than adequate results.

## GLOSSARY OF INGREDIENTS

**BAMBOO SHOOTS:** Canned whole bamboo shoots are readily available. To get rid of any tin flavor prior to using, drain them and boil in water for 2 minutes. (Stay away from canned sliced or chopped shoots, as getting rid of the tin flavor is just about impossible.) If you can find them, the best whole shoots are precooked and vacuum-sealed. They are sold in Japanese and Korean markets, and occasionally in Chinese markets. Fresh or frozen shoots are also excellent, but they require more prep time. You will need to remove the sheaths (leaves) and boil them for 15 minutes prior to using them to get rid of natural toxins.

**BOK CHOY:** Readily available, this Chinese cabbage has broad, dark green leaves and a white or light green stem. Be sure to buy them small rather than large. The Chinese value young vegetables for their tenderness. The more mature the vegetable, the more fibrous and less desirable it is.

**BONITO FLAKES:** Found in Japanese and Korean markets and in health foods stores, bonito flakes are paper-thin flakes of dried tuna. They are used for making dashi (Japanese Kelp Stock, page 51).

**CHILI-GARLIC SAUCE:** Chili-garlic sauce is as readily available as soy sauce and fish sauce. This bright red sauce can be chunky or smooth. The smooth kind is labeled "sriracha" and is sold in a bottle with a squirt top.

**CHRYSANTHEMUM LEAVES:** Also referred to as garland chrysanthemum or edible chrysanthemum, these serrated leaves can be dark green and narrow or rounded and broad. Found in Japanese or Korean markets, they impart a floral note to any number of dishes, such as soups and stir-fries. They can also be added to a salad mix, such as mesclun.

**CILANTRO:** Also known as Chinese parsley, cilantro is dark green with tender leaves and stems, both of which are used in cooking. If a recipe instructs you to trim cilantro, cut out off about 1/2 to 1 inch of the stem and get rid of any bruised stems or leaves.

**CINNAMON:** It is occasionally used in Asian cooking, mostly in braised foods and for flavoring stocks. Chinese and Vietnamese cinnamon, which is made from the bark of cassia trees, is sweeter and more fragrant than Ceylon cinnamon. Although Ceylon cinnamon is more readily available, you may find Vietnamese cinnamon (labeled "Saigon cinnamon") among the spices at the supermarket. Either type can be used for the recipes here.

**COCONUT MILK:** Choose canned unsweetened coconut milk. Many Asian cooks buy this product to save themselves the time and effort required to make their own. Canned coconut milk labeled "lite" is unnecessary. It is watered down coconut milk. You can dilute regular coconut milk with as much or as little water as you wish.

**CORNSTARCH:** Derived from corn kernels, cornstarch is used to thicken sauces and occasionally soups. (Tapioca starch, described below, is another thickener.)

**CURRY PASTE:** This wet curry paste is a Thai ingredient that comes in red, green, and yellow. It is essential to Thai cooking. Red curry paste is the most widely available one, and is what you will need here. Spicy with chilies and fragrant with lemongrass, galangal, ginger, garlic, and kaffir lime leaves, the premade curry paste is now available in supermarkets. It is more than adequate and produces delicious foods, so there is no need to make your own.

**CURRY POWDER:** Much less spicy but just as fragrant as a Thai curry paste, dry curry powder is essential in Indian cooking. It can be added to stir-fries to enhance the color and flavor of a dish, such as Singapore Noodles (page 117).

**DARK SESAME OIL:** This dark, honey-colored oil is used sparingly to deepen the flavor of any number of Asian foods. It can be used in marinades, dipping sauces, or as a last-minute flavor enhancer. A small amount will go a long way, so be sure to add a dash at a time; the flavor can overwhelm the palate.

**DILL (FRESH):** The seeds of this herb are associated with pickles rather than Asian foods. Fresh dill is widely used in

Vietnamese cooking, however. Generous quantities flavor a special dish of rice vermicelli and fried fish. Use the fresh feathery leaves and stems.

**DRIED SHRIMP:** Widely used in Chinese and Southeast Asian cuisine, dried shrimp come in various sizes in clear packages, which are labeled XS, S, M, or L. These can be found in Asian markets and in Mexican markets, too. Stay away from dull-colored shrimp or those displaying more shell than meat. Look for plump, pink, vibrant shrimp when selecting. Fish sauce can be used to enhance the flavor of a dish if dried shrimp are not available.

**DRIED SQUID:** Used to deepen the flavors of stock or munched on as a snack, dried squid range in size from small to large, with a few sizes in between. Before snacking on the squid or using it in a stock, be sure to remove the thin skin. To do this, blacken the skin slightly by moving the squid back and forth over an open flame, turning it once, until slightly charred. When cool enough to handle, remove the skin. Dried squid flavors the Southeast Asian Pork and Seafood Stock (page 48). It is available in Asian markets. Use fish sauce if dried squid is too difficult to find.

**FISH SAUCE:** This sauce is made of salted anchovies that have fermented in wooden barrels or earthenware containers for 12 to 15 months. Fish sauce is imported from Thailand mostly, but also from Vietnam and the Philippines. When purchased, it should be clear and honey-colored. Once the bottle has been opened, fish sauce will start darkening and developing salt crystals, which sink to the bottom of the bottle. When no longer golden, and close to soy sauce in color, it is past its prime, much too salty to use, and should be replaced. Diluting it with water will not help. Buy this sauce in small quantities, or only as much as you think you will use within 6 months, for the very best flavor.

**FIVE-SPICE POWDER:** Found in health food stores and increasingly in supermarkets, Chinese five-spice powder actually contains more than five spices, including star anise, cinnamon, Szechuan peppercorns, cloves, and ginger. It also contains tangerine peel. (The mix varies somewhat, depending on the manufacturer.) The "five" in five-spice powder represents nature's five elements: water, metal, fire, earth, and wood.

**GARLIC:** Mildly spicy, garlic is very important to the Asian diet. It is crushed, sliced, or minced, depending on the recipe and how much the individual cook wants it to impact the final dish.

**GINGER:** Used in great quantity, this rhizome (a stem that grows beneath the soil) is believed by many to be a cure-all. In Asian cultures it is used in just about every meal. Look for firm, light-colored pieces. When young the skin is translucent, revealing the pale yet vibrant yellow color of the tender and juicy rhizome. Young ginger is used for making Japanese pickled ginger. When mature, the skin is opaque and grayish-beige in color, and the rhizome is much more fibrous than its young counterpart. If mature, the flesh should still be a vibrant yellow color. If the flesh is gray, discard the ginger. In general, grate for marinades or sauces, slice or crush for stocks and stews, and finely julienne for stir-frying and garnishing.

**HOISIN SAUCE:** This sauce is a thick, dark brown, sweet and salty, fermented soybean paste of Chinese origin. It appears in many Chinese dishes, and is used in Vietnam as a condiment for *pho* (see page 121) as well.

**KELP:** The word describes several types of brown algae, but usually refers to Japanese *kombu*, or giant kelp. It is used to flavor soups and stocks, including the vegetarian stock *Kombu Dashi* (see Japanese Kelp Stock, page 51). Kelp can also be deep-fried and eaten like chips, a delicious and relatively healthful snack.

**LEMONGRASS:** Widely available fresh or frozen, lemongrass gives a delicious lemony flavor to any dish without the tanginess associated with lemons. To trim, remove the bruised outer leaves, root ends, and tough green tops before using. After trimming, about 8 to 10 inches of the stalk (the creamy white and light green parts) can be used. If you can grow your own lemongrass, do so. It is easy, and you'll be able to use the fresh leaves of this tall grass to flavor stocks.

**LIME:** A citrus fruit especially enjoyed in Southeast Asian cuisine for its tangy and bitter notes. Use lemons if limes are not available.

**MINT:** There are many types of mint, but the ones most readily available are peppermint and, occasionally, spearmint. A spearmint leaf is broad with serrated edges, while a peppermint leaf (a hybrid of spearmint, actually) is slightly narrower. Asians tend to use only fresh mint leaves.

**MIRIN:** This is essentially a thin simple syrup made with sugar and rice wine. It can be used to enhance and sweeten sauces and salad dressings.

**MUNG BEAN SPROUTS:** These sprouts have tiny yellow heads attached to thin white stems, which are juicy and crisp. They are often used to garnish any number of soups or stir-fries. Soybean sprouts, which have larger yellow heads, make a perfect substitute.

**OYSTER SAUCE:** Made from oyster extract, this savory and slightly sweet sauce is used in marinades and sauces. In addition, it is sometimes poured straight from the bottle onto steamed or blanched vegetables, such as Chinese broccoli.

**PEANUT OIL:** Peanut oil is widely used as an Asian cooking ingredient. Also known as groundnut oil (and sometimes labeled as such), it is a high-temperature cooking oil ideal for stir-frying and deep-frying. Grapeseed oil is another high-temperature cooking option.

**PRESERVED CHINESE CABBAGE:** This finely chopped Napa cabbage is preserved with salt and packed in earthenware. Called Tien Sin cabbage, after the name of the province it comes from in China, this specialty item is available in Asian markets. There is no substitute for this ingredient.

**PRESERVED DAIKON:** Daikon strips are preserved in salt and sugar. Light beige and chewy, they are used to flavor all sorts of food. There is no substitute for this ingredient, which is found primarily in Asian markets.

**RICE VINEGAR:** Clear or pale gold in color, rice vinegar is mild in flavor and is available plain or "seasoned." I suggest you start with the plain type and season the dish according to your personal preference. If using mildly sweet and salty seasoned rice vinegar, adjust the seasoning of the dish accordingly.

**RICE WINE:** Chinese Shaoxing wine and Japanese sake are both rice wines, and they are used in similar ways, for example to enhance marinades, sauces, and soup stocks. That said, each is distinct in flavor and visually different. Shaoxing wine is consistently golden in color while sake is clear to cloudy white, the latter being too special and expensive to cook with. Rice wine is not to be confused with rice alcohol, which is a spirit with a high alcohol content. While Shaoxing wine may not be available in every liquor store, sake is and can be used in any recipe in this book that calls for rice wine.

**SCALLIONS:** Also known as green onions and bunching onions, scallions are widely used in Asian cooking and appear in many dishes as either a fresh or fried garnish. In general you can crush scallions with the side of a knife and add them to stock, chop them for a stir-fry, or mince them and add to marinades—but it all depends on the cook and the recipe.

**SHIITAKES (DRIED AND FRESH):** There are too many varieties of shiitake mushrooms to count. The most widely available are dried, thin, dark brown, and slightly chewy when cooked. Fairly inexpensive, dried shiitakes, often labeled "black mushrooms" in Asian markets, impart an interesting roasted or fermented flavor to any dish. So fragrant are these mushrooms that the colonial French called them *champignons parfumés,* meaning "perfumed mushrooms." By contrast, the fresh mushrooms (at least the ones most widely available on the market) tend to be mild in flavor and tender. Be sure to soak dried shiitakes in plenty of room temperature or cold water until fully rehydrated and soft, about 30 minutes. Make sure the mushrooms are completely softened, even if it takes more time.

**SOY SAUCE (THIN OR THICK):** Sometimes referred to as "light soy sauce" or simply as "soy sauce," thin soy sauce is used to season food. (It is not the same as *lite* soy sauce, which usually indicates a low-sodium version.) Thick soy sauce, which contains molasses, is used mainly as a food colorant. As noted earlier, soy sauce should be replaced within 1 year, even if you don't notice any deterioration.

**STAR ANISE:** Available in health food stores and some supermarkets, star anise is dark brown and quite literally resembles a star, hence the name. Similar in flavor to anise seeds (which can be used as a substitute), it imparts a sweet licorice flavor to foods.

**TAMARIND:** This is available fresh, in blocks of pulp, as a concentrated liquid, or as a paste. Look for the concentrated liquid or paste because these can be used instantly. The recipes in this book call for the concentrated liquid. If using the paste, halve the quantity. The fresh tamarind and blocks of pulp require time-consuming prep work (such as removing the brittle pod, fibers, and seeds, combining the pulp with water to soften it, and finally pressing the loosened pulp though a fine-mesh sieve). Tamarind will provide a tangy and subtly sweet flavor to any dish. It is a souring agent, so in a pinch, use the juice of a lemon for a different but still tangy flavor.

**TAPIOCA STARCH:** Like cornstarch (see above), tapioca starch is used as a thickener. It is derived from the yucca (also known as cassava) root.

**THAI BASIL:** Available in Asian markets and occasionally in health food stores, Thai basil has a delicious floral note reminiscent of licorice. It is often added to foods as a last-minute garnish. In a pinch, use cilantro for a very different, but still authentically Asian flavor.

**THAI CHILIES:** A key ingredient in some Asian dishes, and as a table condiment, Thai chilies can be red, yellowish-orange, orange, or green. I always choose red because its vibrant color looks beautiful in dishes. In a pinch I have also used fresh cayenne pepper or Scotch bonnets, which are hotter. For every Thai chili, use only about a quarter of a Scotch bonnet. A cayenne pepper is at least twice as big as a Thai chili and is equally hot.

**TIGER SHRIMP:** These plump, firm shrimp get their name from the black stripes on their shells. They are referred to as black or blue tiger shrimp. Gulf shrimp are a delicious alternative in a pinch.

**TOGARASHI PEPPER:** This Japanese chili pepper mix is available in Asian markets and health food stores. In a pinch, use cayenne pepper powder, but do so sparingly because it is much hotter than togarashi (also known as *shichimi-togarashi*).

**WASABI:** When fresh, this pungent ingredient is finely grated into a beautiful light green paste. It is used to spice up tamari or soy sauce and is also served alongside sushi or with soba noodles. Referred to as Japanese horseradish, fresh wasabi is very expensive, often about $10 per ounce. The next best option is dry wasabi powder. Mix 2 parts wasabi powder to 1 part water to form a paste, and roll it between the palms of your hands until it comes off easily, leaving your hands clean, and ensuring a proper consistency.

# BASIC EQUIPMENT AND TECHNIQUES

CHAPTER 2

For millenia, many marvelously efficient Asian home cooks have prepped their ingredients with rudimentary implements. They worked comfortably with a single pot and knife, developing the foods we enjoy today. While you have more than a pot and knife at your disposal, try to keep it simple and always use the equipment with which you are most comfortable.

Before you contemplate buying the Asian cooking equipment described below, you should have a large stockpot, sauté pan, cookie sheet for baking, and a chef's knife. A pairing knife, peeler, mandoline, and grater will also be useful.

If you plan on doing a lot of Asian cooking, then invest in basic and very inexpensive Asian cooking equipment, including a wok, clay pot, bamboo steamer, all-purpose cleaver, and a santoku knife, which is often described as an Asian chef's knife. These can be purchased at an Asian market or online. If you can buy them in person, do so. You will be able to see, touch, and feel the equipment, and get a sense of how they feel in your hand. The descriptions below will help you make the right choices.

Now I am going to get up on my soapbox here for a bit: In order to enjoy your cooking experience more, I encourage you to take a course on knife skills. Good knife skills will help you become an efficient cook. You will get that much more pleasure out of your cooking because the prep, a big part of Asian cooking, will seem effortless. If you can't take a course in person, find some online videos (search the Web under "knife skills") or read some books, such as *In the Hands of a Chef: The Professional Chef's Guide to Essential Kitchen Tools* (Culinary Institute of America, 2007). Most courses, whether online or at a local cooking school, cover basics such as holding the knife and food items properly, moving around in the kitchen safely with a knife (blade down), and what to look for in a good knife. The online videos cover the basics in only a few minutes, and it is time well spent.

## BASIC ASIAN COOKING EQUIPMENT

### Woks

Used for stir-frying, deep-frying, and steaming, the best woks are made of spun carbon steel. They are available in several sizes; the most functional woks measure 14 to 16 inches in diameter. This large size is ideal for supporting large bamboo steamers, which are perfect for steaming several buns or dumplings at a time. A large wok is also great for stir-frying, allowing the cook plenty of tossing room. Good inexpensive woks can be found in Chinatowns everywhere, in kitchen supply stores, or online.

**COOKING WITH A WOK**   Wok cooking requires high temperatures. In fact, it is not unusual for restaurant woks to be heated to 300,000 BTUs per burner. Most home stoves will output 8,000 to 15,000 BTUs of heat per burner, by comparison. It is a huge difference! To ensure that your wok is hot enough during cooking, it is important to preheat it on high heat until it starts to smoke. Only then should you add cooking oil or your preferred fat and start stir-frying. When you stir-fry, keep all the ingredients moving by stirring constantly with cooking chopsticks or a spatula (or both) to prevent burning (hence the term "stir-frying"). The high temperature heat should be distributed evenly throughout the wok as you stir-fry. The only way to ensure this is to make sure the wok is not too crowded—about a third full as a general rule—and to continuously toss the ingredients until everything is cooked through.

**ROUND- VERSUS FLAT-BOTTOMED WOKS** Woks with rounded bottoms were originally designed to be used directly over charcoal braziers. The rounded bottom sat securely in a charcoal well. These woks were also used in old wood-fired stoves with a built-in round hole specifically designed to receive the wok.

Round-bottomed woks can work fine on top of many gas-stove burners, or on an open flame. They don't sit stably on flat burners, particularly electric or induction burners, however. This is why many woks come with a diffuser, also called a wok ring. While the narrow side of the diffuser sits directly on the burner, the wider side supports the wok.

Woks with flat bottoms are especially useful on electric stoves. These sit directly and stably on top of the coil or the flat heated surface.

**CARBON VERSUS STAINLESS AND OTHER CONSIDER-ATIONS** When choosing a round-bottomed wok, I like to go for the relatively large spun carbon steel ones. They work very well and are surprisingly inexpensive, starting at about $20. Like cast-iron cookware, they should be cured.

Before curing your wok, wash it to get rid of factory oil. To cure your wok and maintain it, I suggest the following:

When cooking, use plenty of oil, especially the first few times while the wok builds up a patina, which eventually will become nonstick. Immediately after stir-frying, sprinkle the cooking surface with coarse salt and let the wok absorb any cooking residue while you enjoy your meal. Then rinse the wok under hot running water and return it to the stove. Fire up the burner to dry the wok completely and to prevent it from rusting. When the wok is cool enough to handle, dampen a clean paper towel with cooking oil and rub a very light coating over the cooking surface of the wok. Put it away until the next time. Follow the same routine when using your wok to steam food. (An oil-cured wok will darken with each use. This is normal—enjoy your hard-earned patina!)

A stainless steel wok will never build up a patina. It's literally stainless. Generally these fancy, expensive woks are flat on the bottom. A stainless steel wok can be cared for in the same manner as any stainless steel cookware. Soapy water and a good rinse under hot water will do for cleaning.

Woks come with a single long handle or two short rounded handles on opposite sides. I prefer the two-handle option because it is easier to work with, and certainly to move or carry when you have food inside. Make sure the wok comes with a wok ring, if it has a round bottom, and a lid. Some woks also come with a cooking spatula and a draining rack for deep-frying. The rack is attached directly to the inside of the wok, so when you drain the deep-fried morsels, the excess oil falls to the bottom.

I have avoided describing nonstick woks here because I have reservations about using nonstick pans at a high heat.

Cured carbon steel and stainless steel woks will generally not stick when used properly.

## Clay Pots

Chinese clay pots are great for making stocks and braising foods. I always make braised cellophane noodles in a clay pot, which yields perfect results—slightly chewy noodles and tender morsels of cabbage and mushrooms, for example. Clay pots should be used over an open flame, so gas stoves are ideal for cooking with these vessels.

When selecting a clay pot, be sure it is free of any cracks that may have occurred during shipment. Generally a Chinese clay pot is made of a mixture of fine sand and clay. Sometimes called a sand pot, it is usually beige and unglazed on the outside and glazed in a rich, glossy reddish-brown, brown, black, or blackish-blue coating on the inside. If you can feel the somewhat grainy texture of the sandy clay through the glaze, it is not a good glaze—avoid it. The glaze should be thick and smooth. Because clay pots are fragile, some manufacturers encase them in a wire frame or net. This helps protect the pot by allowing cooking heat to distribute evenly.

A small clay pot for making sauces should cost about $4, a medium one about $8, and a large one about $12, give or take a few. There are several sizes and styles, so have fun browsing the clay pot section of your Asian market. Some clay pots come with a single short handle, others with double handles set on opposite sides. Either will do.

To cure the pot initially, soak it in water overnight. Then dry the outside, fill the pot with water, and put it on a burner set on very low heat and bring the water to a simmer. Gradually increase the heat to medium and eventually to high and boil the water until it has reduced by a half to two-thirds. (You can also place the water-filled pot in the oven, bringing both pot and oven up to 250°F, and reduce the liquid.) Repeat this step a second time to remove any sandy clay smell or taste. Do not be alarmed, however, if after going through this exercise your pot still smells of sand and clay. Eventually, after cooking with the pot several times, the smell will disappear entirely.

Cleaning clay pots is relatively easy. Be sure to wash the pots in very light soapy water and rinse under running hot water after every use. If the cooking residue does not come off easily, fill the pot with water and slowly bring it to a boil. Similar to a deglazing cooking technique, the hot water should help the residue come off easily.

Clay pots are temperature sensitive, and sudden temperature shifts will crack them. Here are some tips:

1. Make sure the clay pot is at room temperature before placing it over an open flame. If you have refrigerated leftovers in the pot, for example, be sure to bring the pot and its contents up to room temperature before heating it. Start with a low flame and gradually increase the heat.

2. Never put an empty clay pot over an open flame to preheat it. A clay pot should always contain food or liquid before it is placed over the heat.

3. It is essential that the pot be heated slowly, or it will crack. To stir-fry garlic and ginger in a clay pot, for example, first place the oil, garlic, and ginger in the pot, then

place the pot over low heat, gradually increasing the heat to medium and then high.

4. Never place a hot clay pot on a cold surface or put it directly into the refrigerator without cooling. Again, sudden temperature shifts will damage your pot.

## Asian Steamers

**BAMBOO STEAMERS** Bamboo steamers are perfect for steaming dumplings and buns. They are inexpensive and come in several sizes, but the only size you really need is a large one that will fit inside your wok. A bamboo steamer for a 14- to 16-inch wok will measure about 12 inches in diameter, for example. The steamers usually come with two stackable steaming racks and a lid.

The first time you use a bamboo steamer, wash it in slightly soapy water and rinse it under hot running water. With each use the bamboo will darken, and eventually achieve a rich golden patina. Caring for a bamboo steamer is easy. First, always line the steamer racks with lettuce or Napa cabbage leaves. The food, including buns or dumplings, should be placed on these leaves and never directly on the rack to keep the racks clean between batches. Second, wash the racks under running hot water after every use.

**STAINLESS STEEL STEAMERS** Stainless steel steamers have the same round shape as their bamboo cousins and can be cared for in the same manner as any stainless steel cookware. To steam buns and dumplings, always line the racks with lettuce or Napa cabbage leaves first, just as you would in a bamboo steamer, to keep the racks clean between batches.

## Chinese Cleavers

The Chinese cleaver is the knife of choice for Asian home cooks and restaurant chefs alike. It is my preferred knife as well because its wide blade allows for greater accuracy and consistency, especially in slicing. Chopping is also fast and easy. The blade, heavier than that of a French-style chef's knife, falls back onto the food so effortlessly that ingredients are finely chopped in no time at all. Some Asian chefs will use two cleavers for mincing meat, which allows them to control the texture and gives much better results than meat ground with commercial machines. (The machines process the meat too finely.) When you make the filling for dumplings, I encourage you to "grind" your own meat with an all-purpose cleaver (see page 32).

I will not discuss Japanese knives here other than to say that they are generally much too expensive for the average cook. On the low end each blade can cost a couple hundred dollars and on the high end several thousand. Japanese knives are highly specialized and need careful handling with great skill. Unless you are a professional chef, are comfortable with many specialized types of Asian knives designed for specific tasks, and are very skillful and precise, I recommend you steer clear of Japanese knives. A mass-manufactured Japanese-style santoku, which costs about $75, is all you will need unless you are a master. A santoku is easier for smaller hands to use than a typical chef's knife because the santoku blade is about 7 inches long and 2 inches high. The Japanese santoku is derived from the Chinese carving cleaver, which is used for slicing meat or vegetables.

**ALL-PURPOSE CLEAVER** An Asian cook will always have an all-purpose cleaver, which is used for slicing, mincing, and chopping all sorts of ingredients and for cutting through poultry bones. It has a short wooden handle and a 3-inch-high blade, about 7 inches long. It is the most versatile of the three types of cleavers listed here. One of these can replace a full set of Western kitchen knives. The classic Chinese version can cost as little as $6 and as much as $125 for a high-end model made in Europe.

**CARVING CLEAVER** This cleaver, with its 2-inch-high, 7-inch-long blade, resembles the above-mentioned Japanese santoku. It ranges from $4 to about $25 or more for European-made models. Like the all-purpose cleaver, it has a short, round wooden handle. It is used for carving meat, such as Peking duck, and for slicing and dicing meats and vegetables.

## THE PREP

Anyone interested in becoming a better and more efficient home cook should find the following techniques and suggestions helpful.

### Mis-en-place

This French term literally means "put in place." It refers to the practice of organizing the ingredients needed for a specific recipe and having them fully prepped and measured out before going near the stove. The last thing you want to do is heat the oil in a skillet, then run to your chopping board to mince garlic. By the time you get back to the skillet, the oil will be so hot it will either smell bad or burn the garlic upon initial contact. *Mis-en-place* is the standard practice in Asian cooking: prep first, then head for the heat.

### Julienne

This is a technique for slicing something very thinly. In Asian cooking julienned ingredients are transformed into fine, delicate strands, and that is what I mean when I call for an ingredient to be julienned. To julienne an item, for example ginger, thinly slice it into broad, paper-thin slices or planks and then stack the planks and slice again lengthwise. Proper knife skills, practice, and patience make perfect here.

### Chopping

There are gradations of chopping: *coarsely chopped*, *chopped*, *finely chopped*, and *minced*. Consider the peanut: If

you quartered it, it would be *coarsely chopped*. If cut into
8 to 12 pieces, it would be considered *chopped,* and if cut
into 20 pieces, *finely chopped*. When granulated, it would
be *minced*.

### Freezing and Slicing Meat

To achieve fine, paper-thin slices, place a block of meat in
the freezer for 30 to 45 minutes before slicing it. It will turn
a difficult task into an easy, manageable one, especially if
you are using a cleaver.

### Precooking and Soaking Noodles

When cooking wheat, egg, buckwheat, or rice noodles
in broths, note that the noodles should first be boiled in
water to remove the excess flour coating and, occasionally,
a yellow food coloring. They are never directly added to a
broth for cooking. Once boiled, they are set in a soup bowl
and the broth is ladled or poured over them. This proce-
dure will ensure that your broth remains clear and beautifully presentable.

Rice noodles, rice paper, and cellophane noodles should be
soaked in water to cover until pliable to ensure even cooking and proper texture before precooking (if necessary) and
then braising or stir-frying.

### Soaking Dried Shiitakes or Cloud Ears

Dried fungus should be soaked in water to cover until fully
rehydrated and softened, which on average takes between
20 and 30 minutes, depending on the size or thickness
of the mushrooms. Squeezing them between the palms
of your hands will remove excess water. Discard shiitake
stems and use only the caps.

### Removing Fat from Stock

Any of these techniques will work. Pick one and repeat as
many times as is necessary to remove most or all of the fat.

1. Lower a ladle so it sits on the surface of the stock. Angle
   it to catch the fat—while preventing the stock from get-
   ing into the ladle—and discard.

2. Place a paper towel on the surface of the stock, lift (the
   fat will cling to the paper towel), and discard.

3. Refrigerate the stock for several hours until the fat solidifies. With a spoon, lift the solid fat and discard.

### Freezing Stocks

Make stocks in large quantities and freeze them in two
sizes for later use: 1-cup or 1-pint containers for making
sauces, and 1-quart containers for soup.

# BASIC CONDIMENTS AND STOCKS

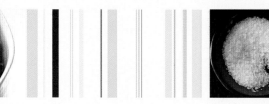

CHAPTER 3

Table condiments and garnishes are an integral part of any dining experience in Asia. Broadly analogous to Western salt and pepper, they are much more critical to the meal and more integrated into the ritual of dining. It is often said that you should taste the food before seasoning it at a Western table, so as not to offend the chef. The opposite is true at many Eastern tables—you season so as *not* to offend the chef! So while Asian noodles are delicious as prepared, a little flavor enhancer such as Fried Scallions in Oil (page 40) or chili-garlic sauce, for example, is welcomed as an on-the-spot food and flavor adjustment. But the Eastern custom goes beyond flavor. Asian diners are expected to season and garnish their own serving of food at the table in order to participate in the meal. This concept goes back to the notion that the chef should not be taken for granted, and that diners should show gratitude before consuming the food by participating in these minor rituals. Besides, in many instances, the chef will have selected the condiments and freshly made the garnishes especially for the meal.

There are many different Asian condiments and garnishes. A Vietnamese restaurant might routinely have half a dozen or so at the table, for example. I provide recipes for a few basic ones that are easy to make with readily available ingredients. You will be able to use these to raise your noodle "snack" to the level of a sophisticated flavor experience. For example, Fried Garlic in Oil (page 39), Fried Scallions in Oil (page 39), and Fried Shallots (page 39) make for wonderful garnishes, lending any stir-fry or soup a fragrant, roasted, sweet finish. The Sweet, Sour, and Spicy Fish Sauce (page 41) will enhance a fried spring roll with notes of tangy lime, spicy chilies, pungent garlic, and salty fish sauce, refreshing the palate after every bite. Note that these wonderful items are often served in their own festive little dishes, adding color and a sense of adventure to the table.

Although I call for specific condiments in some noodle recipes, feel free to experiment by adding other ones. And if I have not specified any, but you would enjoy a little something extra on your noodles, feel free to browse the recipes in the next few pages for inspiration.

Marinades are important here too, because seasoning proteins before they're added to a stir-fry is a common practice in Asia. For this purpose, I've included Basic Asian Marinade (page 43), made with soy sauce, sesame oil, garlic, ginger, and scallion. If you're too tired to fuss in the kitchen after a long day at work, this recipe makes enough for the week. Just use a different cut of meat or seafood each night along with a different noodle (egg, wheat, or buckwheat, for example) and you will be awash in enough varied flavors and textures to satisfy even jaded diners. You'll be able to get dinner on the table faster than the take-out pizza guy, and your interpretation of Asian "fast food" will be more healthful than Chinese fast food.

In addition to condiments, I also include easy-to-make stocks. You will find the most basic Asian chicken, pork, or beef stock flavored with ginger and scallion (page 46), and more complex ones, such as Southeast Asian Pork and Seafood Stock (page 48), made with dried squid, preserved daikon, and star anise. And for those who really do want and have the time to venture off to Chinatown for ingredients, Japanese seaweed stock called dashi (page 51) is also included. This stock is necessary for the preparation of many Japanese-style noodle soups and sauces.

Integral to much Asian food preparation, stocks are used for making soups and sauces, and for braising foods. Although they require very little preparation time, they do simmer for several hours, which is key in developing deep, complex flavors. As a result, when I set out to make stock, I turn it into a big project and then freeze the stock in two sizes: 1-pint containers for making sauces, and 1-quart containers for making soups. Preparing some of these basic stock recipes is an excellent way to turn a slow or boring day into a very productive one; any of them can be made ahead of time and refrigerated or frozen for later use. When freezing, be sure to date the containers and use within 3 months. If you have defrosted a container of stock, but found that you did not make use of all or any of it, reheat it to a gentle boil prior to returning the unused portion to the freezer.

A helpful hint: Invite friends over and turn your kitchen into a stock-making assembly line. Everyone gets to shop, prep, and cook together and then take some home. And you can do whatever you like while the pots simmer.

# FRIED GARLIC IN OIL

**Makes about 2 cups**

Fried Garlic in Oil is a perfect complement to any number of noodle soups. Medium gold in color, it adds a toasted and sweet character to any food it comes into contact with. Note that the amount of oil required will vary, depending on the size of the garlic head. The trick is to make sure that the finely chopped garlic is leveled and is covered by about ⅛ inch of oil. When making fried garlic oil, it is important not to burn the garlic, or it will taste bitter. Fried garlic oil can be kept refrigerated in an airtight jar for up to 1 week for the best flavor.

¾  cup vegetable oil

3  garlic heads, cloves peeled, crushed, and minced

Combine the oil and garlic in a small saucepan and fry the garlic over medium heat until golden, 7 to 10 minutes. Turn off the heat; the garlic will continue to sizzle for a while. Cool completely in the pan and transfer the garlic and flavored oil to a glass jar with a lid.


# FRIED SHALLOTS

**Makes about 2 cups**

Fried Shallots have long been associated with Vietnamese food. They're added to the famous rice noodle and beef soup called *pho* (page 121) and countless other dishes for the sweet flavor and crunchy texture they provide. Unlike Fried Garlic in Oil (above), the fried shallot rings are drained, and the fragrant oil is reserved for other uses, such as stir-frying. Fried Shallots should be well drained on paper towels, then stored in an airtight container in the refrigerator for up to 2 weeks.

1  cup vegetable oil

6  large shallots, halved lengthwise and thinly sliced crosswise into half-moons

In a small saucepan, heat the oil over medium heat. When the oil is hot, add the shallots in small batches (the equivalent of 1 shallot) and fry until golden, about 3 minutes per batch. Use a slotted spoon to remove and transfer each batch to a paper towel–lined plate to drain well and cool. Use immediately or transfer the fried shallots to an airtight container.

# FRIED SCALLIONS IN OIL

**Makes about 1½ cups**

Scallions, or green onions, play as great a role in Asian cuisines as do ginger and garlic. This condiment is often drizzled over rice noodles, adding a deliciously sweet flavor and a bright green color, which contrasts with the stark white noodles. Often the scallions are fried just long enough to infuse the oil, barely changing their color; other times they are fried until pale gold. There is no right or wrong way. It simply depends on the preference of the cook. Fried Scallions in Oil taste best if consumed within 3 days, but can be kept refrigerated in an airtight container for up to 1 week.

¾ **cup vegetable oil**

8 **scallions, trimmed and chopped**

In a small saucepan, heat the oil over medium heat. When the oil is hot, add the scallions, and let sizzle for 1 minute. Turn off the heat (the scallions will continue sizzling for a while) and cool completely in the pan. Transfer the scallions and flavored oil to a container with a lid.

# SWEET, SOUR, AND SPICY FISH SAUCE

**Makes 1½ cups**

This sweet and sour fish sauce dip is made spicy with chopped chilies and garlic, while fresh-squeezed lime or lemon gives it a sour edge. Called *nuoc cham* or *nuoc mam cham* in Vietnamese, it is the ubiquitous condiment of the Vietnamese table. Drizzle it over grilled meat set atop thin rice noodles tossed with shredded vegetables for refreshing fare, perfect for summer.

For a mild sauce, slice the garlic and chilies. For a spicier one, mince them. This sauce will keep for up to 1 week. Bottled fish sauce is the most important ingredient in this recipe. When selecting a bottle, be sure to pick a sauce that is light to medium gold in color. If the fish sauce is too dark (close to or similar to soy sauce in color, and sometimes with salt crystal formations), it is too old and should be avoided or discarded.

½ cup fish sauce

½ cup sugar

½ cup fresh lime or lemon juice

1 large garlic clove, thinly sliced or minced

1 to 2 fresh red Thai chilies, stemmed, seeded, and thinly sliced or minced

In a medium bowl, whisk together the fish sauce and sugar until the sugar is completely dissolved. Stir in the lime or lemon juice and add the garlic and chilies. Let steep for 20 minutes or so before serving. Refrigerate in an airtight container for up to 1 week.

# ASIAN PEANUT SAUCE

**Makes about 3 cups**

2 tablespoons vegetable oil

2 to 3 tablespoons Thai red curry paste, or to taste

1½ cups unsalted dry-roasted peanuts, ground to a powder

¼ cup palm sugar or light brown sugar

2 cups unsweetened coconut milk

2 cups Basic Asian Stock (chicken, page 46)

⅓ cup tamarind (liquid concentrate) or fresh lemon juice

¼ cup hoisin sauce

2 tablespoons fish sauce

½ cup packed fresh cilantro or mint leaves, minced

It is a smart idea to learn how to make a good peanut sauce. For one, it is a great sauce for dipping all sorts of cocktail foods, including the popular fresh spring rolls (also known as summer rolls). Or, try tossing egg noodles with it for a quick bite—I promise that you will not be disappointed. The cooked sauce can be refrigerated for up to 3 days. After refrigeration it may thicken. If that is the case, just add a small amount of water or chicken stock to loosen the sauce while slowly reheating it. You can substitute 1 cup 100 percent pure peanut butter for the peanuts to save time. Some store-bought red curry pastes are spicier than others, so add it according to your taste.

In a saucepan, heat the oil over medium heat. Add the curry paste and stir-fry until fragrant, about 2 minutes. Add the peanuts and stir, roasting them until two shades darker but not burnt, about 8 minutes. Add the sugar and continue to stir until the sugar is dissolved and starts to caramelize, 1 to 2 minutes. Add the coconut milk, chicken stock, tamarind, hoisin sauce, and fish sauce. Reduce the heat to low and simmer the sauce until slightly thickened (look for a *crème anglaise* consistency), allowing the natural oils from the peanuts to surface, about 45 minutes. Turn off the heat and stir in the cilantro. Serve at room temperature.

# BASIC ASIAN MARINADE

Makes about 2½ cups

I always like to keep a good Asian marinade in the refrigerator for my husband. If I am out of town and he has to get dinner on the table for himself and our daughter, the marinade makes it easy for him to throw a quick meal together. He just slices some meat, adds some marinade, and lets the meat marinate while the noodles are boiling. On occasion, he adds it to the wok while stir-frying ground turkey with edamame, which he then tosses with boiled udon. You'll find this marinade will turn simple boiled noodles into a quick and delicious meal. About ¼ cup is plenty for marinating up to 1 pound of sliced meat or for seasoning stir-fried noodles. If using ground meat, there is no need to marinate, just add the marinade as a seasoning while stir-frying the meat. The recipe makes enough marinade for several meals. You can keep the marinade refrigerated in an airtight container for up to 1 week.

1   cup thin soy sauce

1   cup mirin

2   tablespoons dark sesame oil

1   tablespoon rice vinegar

2   tablespoons honey

2   large garlic cloves, minced
    or grated

2   scallions, trimmed and minced

2   ounces ginger, finely grated

1   teaspoon chili-garlic sauce

In a jar, combine the soy sauce, mirin, sesame oil, vinegar, honey, garlic, scallions, ginger, and chili-garlic sauce (if using). Secure with a lid, and shake to mix the ingredients. Refrigerate for up to 1 week.

# ASIAN-STYLE KIRBY PICKLES

**Serves 6**

12 kirby, Persian, or Japanese cucumbers, quartered lengthwise (see Note)

1 tablespoon kosher salt

6 tablespoons sugar

1 cup rice vinegar

1 to 2 red Thai chilies, stemmed, seeded, and halved or coarsely chopped (optional)

I don't know about you, but I like to nibble on sweet, salty, and tangy vegetable pickles with my meals. They help digest food and provide balance during the meal, especially when you are eating starchy foods like noodles. They also whet the appetite, which is probably why they are served the minute you sit down in many Asian restaurants. I call for kirby, Persian, or Japanese cucumbers, all of which are slender when compared to regular cucumbers. Kirby and Persian pickles are 4 to 5 inches long, while Japanese cucumbers are a couple of inches longer. The pickling liquid here is traditionally used for pickling sliced cucumber, carrots, and daikon, so feel free to try these vegetables as well. The amount of pickling liquid may look inadequate, but there will be enough because the cucumbers give up some of their natural water while sitting in the brine.

In a large bowl, toss the cucumbers with the salt. Let stand for 1 hour. Drain, wipe, and transfer them to a large resealable plastic bag.

In a small bowl, whisk together the sugar and rice vinegar until the sugar is completely dissolved. Pour into the large plastic bag containing the cucumbers, and add the chilies (if using). Seal the bag, squeezing any air out. Refrigerate for at least 12 hours. The longer the vegetables macerate, the more pickled they will taste.

**NOTE:** If you like a milder flavor, pickle these small cucumbers whole.

# BASIC ASIAN STOCK (BEEF, PORK, OR CHICKEN)

**Makes about 3 quarts**

3 to 4 pounds raw meaty chicken, pork, or beef bones

1  pound daikon, peeled and cut into 2-inch-thick rounds, or whole white round turnips

4  ounces ginger, sliced and lightly crushed

8  scallions, trimmed and lightly crushed

1  teaspoon white or black peppercorns

**Fish sauce or kosher salt**

Basic Asian Stocks are easy to make. Unlike many classic French stocks, they do not require the cook to roast the meaty bones in the oven prior to making the stock. Instead, all Asian stocks are made with fresh meaty bones, which are first boiled 2 to 3 times in order to get rid of bone or blood particles, most of which rise and collect in the foam at the top. Choose meaty bones such as pork ribs for pork stock, beef short ribs or oxtail for beef stock, or chicken carcasses, necks, and wings for chicken stock. A whole chicken can also be used, but I find it wasteful, and prefer to use prime poultry meat for stir-frying with noodles, and other dishes.

Be sure to cut off any fat or skin prior to adding the meat to the stockpot. I always use fish sauce as a basic seasoning, but you can use salt if you prefer. To enhance the flavor of the stock, ginger, scallion, and daikon (or any white turnip) are added to the pot. Basic stocks are used as a base for fragrant soups and sauces. Freeze the stock in two sizes: 1-cup or 1-pint containers for use in making sauces, and 1-quart containers for use as soup stock.

Bring a large stockpot of water to a boil and cook the meaty bones for 10 minutes to get rid of bone and blood particles. (This step can be omitted when making chicken stock with whole bones, but it is especially useful when using chopped-up bones or when making pork or beef stock.) Drain, reserve the bones, and rinse the pot.

In the same large stockpot, combine the boiled bones with 5 quarts of water. Bring to a boil over high heat. Reduce the heat to low and add the daikon, ginger, scallions, and peppercorns. Season lightly with fish sauce or salt. Simmer, partially covered, for 4 to 5 hours, or until you have about 3 quarts of liquid left, occasionally skimming off any foam on the surface. Strain and discard the solids. Then skim off the fat (see page 33).

# CHINESE SUPERIOR STOCK

**Makes about 3 quarts**

In this stock, chicken provides the basic flavor, which is enhanced with a salt-cured meat, such as Smithfield ham from Virginia. The stock is further layered with the flavors of ginger, scallions, and daikon. Basic chicken stock it is not! Chinese Superior Stock is well worth making in large quantities and freezing in 1-cup or 1-pint containers for making sauces, and 1-quart containers for soups. If you can't find Smithfield ham, use prosciutto ends, which are generally available at the butcher or deli counter. You do not have to soak prosciutto (unlike the ham)—just add the piece, minus the fat and rind, to the stockpot.

3 to 4 pounds raw meaty
    chicken bones

One 4-ounce slice Smithfield ham,
    soaked in water for 24 hours
    and drained

1    pound daikon, peeled and cut
    into 2-inch-thick rounds, or
    whole white round turnips

4    ounces ginger, sliced and lightly
    crushed

8    scallions, trimmed and lightly
    crushed

1    teaspoon white or black
    peppercorns

Kosher salt

Put the chicken bones and ham in a large stockpot. Add 5 quarts water and bring to a boil over high heat. Reduce heat to low, and add the daikon, ginger, scallions, and peppercorns. Simmer, partially covered, for 4 to 5 hours, or until reduced to about 3 quarts of stock, occasionally skimming off any foam from the surface. If necessary, add salt to taste and stir. Strain and discard the solids. Then skim off the fat (see page 33).

# SOUTHEAST ASIAN PORK AND SEAFOOD STOCK

**Makes about 3 quarts**

Pork- and seafood-based stocks are popular in Southeast Asia. Dried squid or shrimp and meaty pork bones make for a delicious combination. Found in Asian markets, dried squid come in different sizes and are prepackaged or sold in large containers by weight. Before using them, you must remove the skin. The best way to do so is to blacken the skin, which enhances the flavor (see page 22). Be sure to choose bright pinkish-orange, medium-to-large dried shrimp. (The clear plastic package will be labeled XS, S, M, or L.) Another key ingredient in this stock—also found in Asian markets—is preserved daikon, which sweetens the stock as it simmers. If you cannot find preserved daikon or dried squid, substitute fish sauce for the dried squid and sugar for the preserved daikon.

3 to 4 pounds raw meaty pork ribs, separated if necessary

1 medium dried squid, about 10 inches long, or ⅓ cup dried shrimp; or 2 to 3 tablespoons fish sauce

1 cup preserved daikon strips, or 1 tablespoon sugar

1 pound fresh daikon, peeled and cut into 2-inch-thick pieces

3 ounces ginger, sliced and lightly crushed

8 scallions, trimmed and crushed

1 teaspoon white or black peppercorns

Kosher salt

Bring a large stockpot of water to a boil and cook the meaty bones for 10 minutes to get rid of bone and blood particles. Drain, reserve the ribs, and rinse the pot well.

Return the pork ribs to the same stockpot. Add 5 quarts of water and bring to a boil over high heat. Reduce the heat to low, and add the squid, preserved daikon, fresh daikon, ginger, scallions, and peppercorns. Simmer, partially covered, for 4 to 5 hours, or until reduced to about 3 quarts, occasionally skimming off any foam. If necessary, add salt to taste and stir. Strain and discard the solids. Then skim off the fat (see page 33).

# VIETNAMESE BEEF STOCK

**Makes about 3 quarts**

Fragrant with cinnamon, cloves, and star anise, this beef stock is the foundation for the famous rice noodle and beef soup known as *pho* (page 121). Meaty beef bones such as oxtail or short ribs are excellent for making the stock. Translucent white beef tendons, which require long and slow cooking, can also be added to the stock in fairly large pieces. When the time comes to serve the soup, remove the meaty bones and tendon from the stock, shred or slice the meat and tendon, and add to the soup when serving. Oxtail and beef tendon can be special-ordered from your butcher.

3 to 4 pounds raw meaty beef bones, such as oxtail or short ribs

1 large yellow onion

8 whole cloves

7 whole star anise

2 four-inch cinnamon sticks

1 pound daikon, peeled and cut into 2-inch-thick pieces

3 ounces ginger, sliced

8 scallions, trimmed and crushed

2 tablespoons fish sauce

1 tablespoon sugar

1 teaspoon white or black peppercorns

Kosher salt

Put the oxtail or short ribs in a large stockpot with enough water to cover. Bring to a boil over high heat and cook for 10 minutes to get rid of bone and blood particles. Drain, reserve the meaty bones, and rinse the pot well.

Return the oxtail or short ribs to the same stockpot, add 5 quarts of water, and bring to a boil over high heat. Reduce heat to low and add the onion studded with the cloves, the star anise, cinnamon, daikon, ginger, scallions, fish sauce, sugar, and peppercorns. Simmer, partially covered, for 4 to 5 hours, until reduced to about 3 quarts, occasionally skimming off any foam from the surface. If necessary, adjust seasoning with salt to taste and stir. Strain and discard solids, reserving the meaty bones to pick on if so desired. Skim off the fat (see page 33).

# JAPANESE KELP STOCK

**Makes 4 quarts**

Seaweed-based stock such as the classic Japanese dashi can be used as a soup base or for making sauces. There are three basic stocks to consider for Japanese-style noodle dishes: *Kombu Dashi,* Primary Dashi, and Secondary Dashi. (See the variations below for Primary and Secondary Dashi.) The simplest stock to make is the vegetarian *Kombu Dashi*, which is *kombu*, or kelp, steeped in water for at least 12 hours at room temperature. The Primary Dashi is the most concentrated of the three and is made with kelp and dried tuna flakes, or bonito flakes, at its base. The Secondary Dashi is a by-product of the Primary Dashi; the kelp and tuna flakes used to make the Primary Dashi are recycled to make a less concentrated stock. The stocks can be used interchangeably; it's a matter of preference. To store the dashi, discard the solids and refrigerate for up to 3 days or freeze for up to 3 months.

**FOR THE KOMBU DASHI**

2   ounces dried kelp, wiped clean

5   quarts spring or filtered water

To make the *Kombu Dashi*, put the package of kelp in a large glass bowl and add the spring or filtered water. Let steep for 12 to 24 hours at room temperature. (The longer the kelp steeps in the water, the more concentrated the stock.) Strain the stock and discard the solids.

## Variations

Primary Dashi: Pour the water into a medium stockpot, and bring to a boil over high heat. Reduce heat to low, add the kelp, and simmer for 30 minutes. Add ½ cup of bonito flakes. When the bonito sinks to the bottom of the pot, pour off the stock (leave the kelp and bonito flakes in the pot if you plan to make Secondary Dashi).

Secondary Dashi: Make the Primary Dashi, reserving the kelp and bonito flakes in the pot. (You can freeze the Primary Dashi that you have made for future use.) Pour 2 quarts of fresh spring or filtered water into the stockpot with the kelp and bonito. Bring to a boil over high heat. Reduce heat to low and simmer for 30 minutes. Strain the stock and discard the solids.

# WHEAT NOODLES

CHAPTER 4

Wheat noodles—made from a basic dough of wheat flour, water, and salt—were originally a specialty from the northern wheat-growing parts of China, where they remain the primary starch in everyday diets. These noodles also appear in virtually every other Asian culture. They are cooked in a wide variety of ways, and are served with simple sauces, meat and fish, and all sorts of vegetables. Wheat noodles are available fresh, precooked, and dried. In northern China, as in the West, wheat is linked with the beginning of agriculture and the establishment of fixed human settlements, with the displacement of hunter-gatherer societies and the beginning of human civilization.

The story of wheat cultivation and preparation is a fascinating tale. In the beginning, humans separated the plant's inner grain from its tough, inedible outer chaff by chewing. This primitive method evolved, however, most likely along these lines: Chewing to separate the parts was replaced by threshing. Grinding the grain with teeth was replaced by grinding with tools. And moisture provided by saliva was eventually replaced by water, in which the wheat grains were soaked. (To this day, bulgur wheat is soaked to make Middle Eastern tabbouleh.) The soaked wheat eventually became wheat paste, which was the basis for the first flat breads. They emerged around 10,000 B.C.E. in the Middle East.

Unleavened flat breads are still central to numerous Asian food cultures today.

The dates for the evolution of noodles are tougher to establish. The earliest written records of Chinese wheat noodle production, in particular, date back to the second half of the Han Dynasty (206 B.C.E. to 220 C.E). Until recently, anthropologists assumed that this is when wheat noodle production was introduced to northern China. The appearance of four-thousand-year-old millet noodles in a jar at the archeological site of Lajia in 2005 (see page 9), however, has now turned the whole noodle-origin theory upside down.

Noodles were originally made by folding, pulling, and stretching a dough into long, thick ropes. To stretch out the rope the noodle maker pulled with both hands and deftly swung the strand up and down like a jump rope. This technique is still used for artisanal noodle production, and it is also offered as an amusement in Chinese noodle restaurants. Probably the most extraordinary view of artisanal noodle making is in the 1994 film *Ermu*, directed by Zhou Xiaowen, in which a woman kneads noodle dough with her feet. Noodles are also made by cutting the dough into strips, much like the Italian artisanal *pasta alla chitara* or *guitarra*, "cut by guitar-like strings."

# WHEAT NOODLE TYPES

## CHINESE WHEAT NOODLES

**CU MIAN:** Thick Chinese wheat noodles similar to Japanese udon. Sold dried, the noodles are usally flat and are available in round, individual portion–size bundles, resembling bird's nests. These noodles generally cook in about 5 minutes.

**LAO MIAN:** A thick wheat noodle sold both fresh and precooked. In the West, it is called more often by its Cantonese name, *lo mien*, than by the Mandarin *lao mian*. It is often served in broth or stir-fried, as in the popular Chinese take-out dish pork *lo mien*. The fresh noodles will cook in about 2 minutes. Precooked noodles should be heated in boiling water for 10 seconds before serving in broth, but they can be added directly to stir-fries.

## JAPANESE WHEAT NOODLES

**SOMEN:** Very thin dried round noodles, about as fine as angel hair pasta. Several single portions of somen are sold in one package. The ribbon around each portion is decorative and should be removed prior to cooking. These cook in about 3 minutes

**UDON (DRIED):** Flat or round, these Japanese wheat noodles are white and are sold as several single portions packaged together. The ribbon around each portion is decorative and should be removed prior to cooking. These cook in about 5 minutes.

**UDON (FRESH):** Thick white noodles that come square, round, or flat. The noodles are actually precooked and only need 10 seconds in boiling water to be reheated before serving in broth, or they can be added directly to stir-fries.

The Chinese like their noodles long. "Longevity noodles" are made as long as possible to promote a healthy, long life. Popular at celebrations such as wedding banquets, on the Chinese New Year, and especially at birthdays, the noodles are stir-fried and served with minimal accompaniment. Fresh long noodles are generally sold loosely rolled or folded in half, and dusted with cornstarch to prevent sticking.

The Japanese are fabled noodle enthusiasts. The noodle's appearance is usually attributed to a Buddhist priest who traveled in northern China in the early ninth century, returning with the knowledge of the wheat noodle that has become known as udon. (The generic word for noodles in Japan is *men* or *menrui*, and is clearly derived from its Chinese name, *mian*.)

Udon remains one of Japan's most popular noodles to this day. Round or flat and always thick, udon are often served in a soy sauce–based broth. They are also dipped in soy sauce and accompanied by a variety of side dishes, including pickles and fish. They are also stir-fried or served with a curry sauce—a favorite Japanese fast food. Somen is a thinner version. It is very delicate; dried somen is perhaps a bit more brittle than Italian angel hair pasta. Somen are available plain, or flavored with pink plum. A particularly fun dish to serve is pink somen in broth—always a conversation starter!

Most Japanese noodles are sold prepackaged as one or more single servings. If you have ever wondered what that little ribbon around the perfectly aligned bunch of noodles is, it's a single portion (remove the ribbon before cooking). I include several Japanese udon and somen recipes here, and you will see that they are most often prepared so that the taste and texture of the noodle item is highlighted.

Korea calls its wheat noodles *myon*. The most popular types are similar to Japanese udon and somen. They are served in broth to create noodle soups known as *guksu*, which are made with the ubiquitous spicy pickled cabbage known as kimchi. *Guksu* also contain fried or sliced hard-boiled egg, vegetables, and meat. *Bi bim guksu*, also a Korean wheat noodle mainstay, combines stir-fried noodles with colorful stir-fried vegetables and egg in a heated stone cooking pot. These are tossed at the last minute with a spicy red chili paste.

## SOME TIPS AND GUIDELINES

In choosing wheat noodles, you want to make sure that your dish will be balanced. A thin noodle, such as Japanese somen, will fare well with delicate vegetables, whereas a thicker noodle, for example udon, will hold up to heavier meat and seafood items. Thin noodles offer less starch, and make a good base for light meals and meals consumed during warm seasons. And the stick-to-your-ribs meals of winter seem to work well with heavier noodles. It's as simple as that.

Remember that the main difference between fresh and dried wheat noodles is the texture. Fresh noodles are slightly chewy; dry noodles are usually less so, though not always. While fresh noodles have enjoyed a certain culinary vogue of late, I think of fresh and dried types as very different products that are equally enjoyable.

That said, fresh and precooked wheat noodles are tougher to find than dried, so when you see them, buy them for a change of pace—if only to experience the subtle but interesting differences in texture and flavor. Chinese, Japanese, and Korean markets have them, as do street vendors in Chinatown; health food stores occasionally do as well. Fresh and precooked varieties last up to 2 days in the refrigerator and are easy to prepare. (Whenever possible I use them the day I buy them, when they are delicate and really at their best.) Note that fresh Chinese wheat noodles tend to be thin and beige, while Japanese udon are thick and white.

# WHEAT NOODLES WITH SPICY GROUND PORK AND CABBAGE SAUCE

**Serves 6**

This dish is derived from the Szechuan specialty known as *dan dan mien*. It is named after the clanging sound of bamboo poles that bounce while balanced on a peddler's shoulders. The dish is sweet, savory, and spicy and is made with thick udon-style noodles, which hold up to the rich and meaty pork-and-peanut sauce perfectly. Chinese sesame paste is the same as Middle Eastern *tahini*. White miso is readily available in health food stores, and makes a good substitute for the not so readily available Chinese fermented soybeans traditionally used in this dish.

In a small mixing bowl, whisk together the sesame paste, sesame oil, miso, vinegar, chili-garlic sauce, and sugar until the sugar is completely dissolved.

Meanwhile make the sauce. In a medium saucepan, heat the vegetable oil over high heat. Stir-fry the garlic and shallot until fragrant and golden, 1 to 2 minutes. Add the ground pork and stir-fry to break it up. Add the cabbage and stir-fry until the meat is cooked through, about 2 to 3 minutes more. Add the stock and soy sauce and bring to a boil. Turn off the heat, stir in the sesame paste mixture, and continue stirring until the sauce is well blended. Cover until ready to serve.

Bring a pot of water to a boil over high heat, and cook the noodles until tender yet firm, about 3 minutes for dried udon, 10 seconds for fresh udon, or 2 minutes for fresh Chinese noodles.

Drain the noodles and divide among large soup bowls or plates. Spoon an equal amount of the pork sauce over each serving, and drizzle lightly with hot chili oil, if using. Garnish with peanuts, sliced scallions, and cilantro leaves, and serve.

2 tablespoons sesame paste

2 teaspoons dark sesame oil

2 tablespoons white miso

2 tablespoons rice vinegar

2 to 3 teaspoons chili-garlic sauce

1 teaspoon sugar

1 tablespoon vegetable oil

2 large garlic cloves, minced

1 large shallot, minced

8 ounces coarsely ground pork

8 medium to large Napa cabbage leaves, minced

2 cups Basic Asian Stock (pork or chicken, page 46)

2 tablespoons thin soy sauce

1 pound fresh or 10 to 12 ounces dried udon, or 1 pound fresh Chinese wheat noodles

Hot chili oil (optional)

1/3 cup unsalted roasted peanuts, minced

2 scallions, trimmed and thinly sliced

1 cup cilantro leaves

# WHEAT NOODLES WITH FIVE-SPICE CABBAGE SAUCE AND CRISPY PORK

**Serves 6**

This noodle and pork dish is perhaps best reserved for winter. The fried pork chop, seasoned with a five-spice and salt mix, is served with a similarly seasoned ground-pork-and-cabbage sauce. The sauce is spooned over the flat wheat noodles, and the pork chop is set on top. I stumbled upon this specialty when I walked into an old Chinese restaurant in New York City's Chinatown. It has been in business for decades and the menu has never changed. This is one of my favorite noodle dishes, perfect on a cold winter's day when the weather seems to call for stick-to-your-ribs food.

The chunky sauce is best made a day ahead to give the flavors a chance to develop. Refrigerate the sauce and reheat just before serving.

¼ cup peanut or vegetable oil, plus extra for deep-frying

3 large garlic cloves, finely grated

2 ounces ginger, finely grated

8 ounces coarsely ground lean pork

2½ teaspoons five-spice powder

1 small Napa cabbage, minced

Kosher salt and freshly ground black pepper

2 tablespoons all-purpose flour

6 boneless pork chops, about ¼ inch thick

1 pound fresh or 10 ounces dried udon, or 1 pound fresh Chinese wheat noodles

12 or more sprigs fresh cilantro, stems trimmed

To make the cabbage-and-pork-sauce: In a medium saucepan, heat the ¼ cup of oil over medium heat and stir-fry the garlic and ginger until fragrant. Add the ground pork and 1½ teaspoons of the five-spice powder and stir-fry, breaking up the meat. Cook until the pork is no longer pink, about 3 minutes. Lower the heat, add the Napa cabbage, and season with salt and pepper to taste. Cover the pot and continue to cook, stirring occasionally, until the cabbage becomes very tender, giving up its natural juices, 20 to 25 minutes. Adjust the seasoning to taste, if necessary.

Meanwhile, fill a medium pot halfway with vegetable oil and heat over medium until the temperature reaches 360°F to 375°F for deep-frying. At the same time, bring a medium pot of water to a boil over high heat.

In a small bowl, mix together the remaining teaspoon of five-spice powder, the flour, and salt and pepper to taste. Sprinkle both sides of each pork chop with the spice mixture and deep-fry until golden crisp on both sides and cooked through, carefully flipping the meat once or twice, about 2 minutes total. Drain the chops on a paper towel–lined plate.

Cook the noodles in the boiling water until tender yet firm, about 5 minutes for dried udon, 10 seconds for fresh udon, and 2 minutes for fresh Chinese noodles. Drain and divide the noodles among large soup bowls or plates. Spoon an equal amount of cabbage sauce over each serving of noodles. Top each with a pork chop (sliced, if you wish) and garnish with cilantro.

# WHEAT NOODLES AND VEGETABLE STIR-FRY WITH CRISPY CHICKEN

**Serves 6**

Fried chicken is as popular in Asia as in the United States, and this Asian-style version, fragrant with Chinese five-spice marinade, offers unexpected licorice overtones. One of my favorite ways to fry chicken is in its own fat. No oil is wasted, and the chicken is tender with a crispy skin reminiscent of anything deep-fried without the heavy breading. Served over noodles tossed in a salty scallion-and-ginger oil, the fried chicken can be dipped in chili-garlic sauce for a hot-and-spicy finish. The Asian-Style Kirby Pickles add some salty crunch. There is nothing shy about this dish. The flavors are sharp and bold. A chilled Gewürztraminer wine or an Asian beer, such as Sapporo, Kirin, or Tsingtao, would make a perfect accompaniment.

1½ teaspoons five-spice powder

4 teaspoons kosher salt

1 teaspoon coarsely ground black pepper

6 whole chicken legs (drumsticks and thighs attached)

3 tablespoons vegetable oil

3 scallions, trimmed and minced

1 ounce ginger, finely grated

1 pound fresh or 10 ounces dried udon, or 1 pound fresh Chinese wheat noodles

Asian-Style Kirby Pickles (page 45)

In a small bowl, mix together the five-spice powder, 3 teaspoons of the salt, and the pepper. Season the chicken legs with the dry rub all over. Let stand for 15 minutes at room temperature.

In a large bowl, combine the vegetable oil with the scallions, ginger, and remaining teaspoon of salt. Set the scallion-and-ginger oil aside.

Heat a large nonstick skillet over medium heat. Pan-fry the chicken, skin side down, until crispy, about 7 minutes. Turn the pieces over, cover the pan, and continue to cook until the juices run clear, about 15 minutes. Remove the cover, flip the pieces skin side down again, and finish crisping them, about 3 minutes more. Drain on a paper towel–lined plate.

While the chicken is cooking, bring a medium pot of water to a boil over high heat. Cook the noodles in the boiling water until tender yet firm, about 5 minutes for dried udon, 10 seconds for fresh udon, or 2 minutes for fresh Chinese noodles. Drain, shock under cold running water, and toss the noodles in the scallion-and-ginger oil. Divide among 6 plates and top each with a pan-fried chicken leg. Serve with pickles on the side.

# UDON WITH BRAISED SWEET AND SPICY BEEF SHORT RIBS

**Serves 6**

Beef short ribs are rich, and they make for great winter dishes. Here the short ribs are braised in a caramel sauce spiced with chilies, star anise, and five-spice powder until fork-tender. Green beans are added to the stew and cooked until just tender. The succulent meat and green beans are served over the noodles with some of the braising liquids. If you like, serve Japanese pickled ginger on the side for a delicious counterpoint to the sweet and spicy flavor notes.

The longer it rests, the tastier this dish will be, so braise the ribs the day before you plan to serve them, if possible. I tend to serve less noodles than normal with this hearty dish. The pork butt (shoulder) makes for an equally delicious variation.

¾ cup sugar

⅓ cup rice vinegar

Four 12-ounce bottles amber ale

¾ cup thin soy sauce

3 ounces ginger, thinly sliced

6 dried whole red chilies or fresh red Thai chilies

8 scallions, trimmed and lightly crushed

1 garlic head, cloves peeled and lightly crushed

6 whole star anise

1 teaspoon five-spice powder

4 pounds beef short ribs, or 4 pounds pork butt, cut into large chunks

1 pound green beans, trimmed

1 pound fresh or 8 to 10 ounces dried udon, or 12 ounces fresh Chinese wheat noodles

In a large pot, heat the sugar and vinegar over medium heat, stirring occasionally, until the sugar melts and turns into a rich golden color, 10 to 12 minutes. Add the ale and soy sauce and stir to melt the hardened caramel. Add the ginger, chilies, scallions, garlic, star anise, and five-spice powder and bring to a boil. Reduce the heat to medium-low, add the meat, and simmer partially covered, until the meat is fork-tender or falls off the bones, about 4 hours for short ribs and 2 hours for pork butt.

Before you're ready to serve, scatter the green beans on top of the meat and cook, covered, until tender, 10 to 15 minutes.

Meanwhile, bring a medium to large pot of water to a boil over high heat. Cook the noodles in the boiling water until tender yet firm, about 5 minutes for dried udon, 10 seconds for fresh udon, or 2 minutes for fresh Chinese wheat noodles. Drain. To serve, divide the noodles among individual shallow bowls, and top with the tender braised beef or pork, greens beans, and juices.

# SOMEN NOODLES WITH SHRIMP CURRY AND PEAS

**Serves 6**

Thin wheat noodles, such as Japanese somen, are perfect for light dishes such as this. The bright green color of the peas is complemented by the yellow turmeric-based curry marinade in which the shrimp are cooked. The pungent flavors of garlic and lemon zest offer a subtle, bitter counterpoint to the sweet and tangy character of the dish.

3 tablespoons vegetable oil

1 large garlic clove, minced

1 ounce ginger, finely grated

1 tablespoon Indian curry powder

Juice and grated zest of
2 lemons

Kosher salt and freshly ground
black pepper

10 ounces dried somen

24 small headless tiger shrimp,
peeled, halved lengthwise, and
deveined

1 cup fresh shelled or frozen
green peas, or 1½ cups
edamame (thawed if frozen)

1 scallion, trimmed and thinly
sliced on the diagonal

In a medium bowl combine 1 tablespoon of the oil, the garlic, ginger, curry powder, lemon juice and zest. Season with salt and pepper to taste, add the shrimp, toss, and set aside to marinate for 20 minutes.

Bring a medium pot of water to a boil over high heat. Cook the somen until tender yet firm, about 2 minutes. Shock in ice-cold water. Drain and transfer to a large mixing bowl.

In a large skillet over high heat, add the remaining 2 tablespoons of oil and sauté the shrimp with the marinade for about 1 minute. Add the peas or edamame and toss for 1 minute more. Add the shrimp and peas with their sauce to the noodles. Mix well and divide among large individual bowls or plates. Serve garnished with scallions.

# SOMEN IN BROTH WITH ROMAINE AND CHICKEN TENDERS

**Serves 6**

This noodle soup is made with thin Japanese wheat noodles, called somen; chicken marinated in soy sauce; and blanched romaine lettuce. It is perfect for a chilly spring or autumn night when a light, warm dinner is perfectly suited to the season. Japanese-style soups can be garnished with togarashi, a red chili–based Japanese seasoning mix that includes black pepper, mandarin orange peel, and nori flakes. If you cannot find togarashi, a light sprinkle of cayenne powder will do.

½ cup thin soy sauce

1 tablespoon sugar

1 teaspoon tapioca starch or cornstarch

1 teaspoon dark sesame oil

1 scallion, trimmed and minced

1 pound boneless skinless chicken tenders or breast, thinly sliced

10 cups *Kombu Dashi* (kelp stock, page 51)

½ cup mirin

1 to 2 tablespoons vegetable oil

10 to 12 ounces dried somen

16 large romaine lettuce leaves, torn or cut into large pieces

1 ounce fresh ginger, finely julienned

Toasted sesame seeds for garnish

Togarashi or cayenne powder

In a large bowl, stir together 2 tablespoons of the soy sauce, the sugar, and tapioca starch until the sugar is completely dissolved. Stir in the sesame oil and scallion. Add the chicken and toss to coat evenly. Marinate for 20 minutes.

In a medium pot, pour the kelp stock, the remaining 6 tablespoons of soy sauce, and the mirin and bring to a gentle boil over medium heat. Reduce the heat to low and simmer, covered, until ready to serve.

Meanwhile, heat the vegetable oil in a large skillet or wok over high heat. Stir-fry the chicken until cooked through, about 5 minutes. Transfer to a plate and set aside.

Bring a medium pot of water to a boil over high heat. Cook the somen in the boiling water until tender yet firm, about 3 minutes. Drain and divide the noodles among large soup bowls.

Add the romaine to the broth and cook for 30 seconds. Ladle a generous amount of stock with cooked romaine lettuce over each serving of noodles. Set the chicken atop the noodles and lettuce. Garnish with ginger, sesame seeds, and togarashi to taste.

# UDON WITH VEGETABLE AND SHRIMP TEMPURA

Serves 6

A battered and deep-fried food, tempura was introduced to the Japanese by the Portuguese missionaries in the mid–sixteenth century. The trick with tempura is that the batter has to be cold and lumpy, so don't overmix! I like to add sake or beer to my batter instead of water. It gives the shrimp a little extra and unexpected flavor. Tempura batter is also delicious with all sorts of vegetables, including broccoli, green beans, carrots, and cauliflower. I like colorful meals and often pick my vegetables accordingly. The vegetables and shrimp are generally cooked until barely golden, not brown. To keep the flavors clean, be sure to deep-fry the vegetables before the shrimp, because seafood will add flavor to the oil.

Peanut oil for deep-frying

2   large eggs

¼   cup chilled sake or light beer

1   cup ice water

1¼ cups all-purpose flour

2   quarts Primary or Secondary Dashi (page 51)

2   tablespoons thin soy sauce

2   tablespoons mirin

1   teaspoon dark sesame oil

1   pound fresh or 12 ounces dried udon

2   large carrots, sliced ¼ inch thick on the diagonal

12  medium green beans or broccoli florets

12  medium cauliflower florets

12  medium shiitake mushrooms or cremini mushrooms, stemmed

12  headless jumbo tiger or Gulf shrimp, shelled and deveined

Scallions, trimmed and thinly sliced on the diagonal, for garnish

Toasted sesame seeds for garnish

Togarashi pepper or cayenne pepper (optional)

Fill a medium pot with about 4 inches of peanut oil and heat to 360°F to 375°F.

In a medium to large bowl, lightly beat the eggs with the sake or beer and water. Add the flour all at once, giving it a few stirs. Do not whisk, as the batter should remain lumpy. Refrigerate until ready to use.

In a medium pot, bring the dashi to a gentle boil over medium-low heat. Reduce heat to low, add the soy sauce and mirin, and simmer, covered, until ready to use.

Bring a medium pot of water to a boil over high heat. Cook the udon noodles until tender yet firm, about 5 minutes for dried udon, and 10 seconds for fresh. Drain, and divide among large soup bowls.

Dry the carrots, green beans, cauliflower, mushrooms, and shrimp thoroughly. Working in small batches, dip the vegetables in the batter and deep-fry them until golden on all sides, about 3 minutes. Drain on a paper towel–lined plate. Add the shrimp to the batter and deep-fry them in small batches until opaque and golden, about 2 to 3 minutes. Drain on a paper towel–lined plate.

Ladle about 1¼ cups of stock over each serving of udon. Top with the vegetable and shrimp tempura, and garnish with scallions and sesame seeds. Sprinkle lightly with togarashi, if desired.

# UDON WITH SHIITAKES AND GARLAND CHRYSANTHEMUM LEAVES IN BROTH

**Serves 6**

This vegetarian noodle soup, inspired by many I've had in Japanese restaurants, is made with fresh udon, which are thick and chewy noodles found in the refrigerated section of Japanese and Korean markets. Kelp, a sea vegetable, provides the basic flavor for the stock, which is enhanced with mushroom water, soy sauce, and mirin. The result is a smoky, sweet, and savory broth. Edible chrysanthemum leaves, known as *shingiku* in Japanese, can be found in Japanese, Chinese, and Korean markets. If you can't find them, substitute watercress or a favorite leafy green. Use dried udon if you can't find fresh.

12  small to medium dried shiitake mushrooms, soaked in at least 2½ cups water until pliable

2  quarts *Kombu Dashi* (kelp stock, page 51)

⅓  cup thin soy sauce

⅓  cup mirin

1  pound, preferably fresh, or 12 ounces dried udon

1  large bunch garland chrysanthemum leaves or watercress

2  ounces ginger, finely julienned

Toasted sesame seeds (optional)

Togarashi or cayenne powder (optional)

Drain the mushrooms, reserving 2 cups of the soaking liquid. Discard the stems and quarter the caps.

In a large pot, combine the kelp stock, mushroom liquid, soy sauce, mirin, and shiitakes. Bring to a boil over high heat. Reduce the heat to low and simmer, covered, until ready to serve.

Bring a medium pot of water to a boil over high heat. Cook the fresh udon noodles, untangling them, until separated and warmed, about 10 seconds. (Or boil the dried udon for about 5 minutes.) Drain and divide among large soup bowls.

Add the chrysanthemum leaves to the pot containing the broth, and when just wilted, remove from the heat. Ladle enough broth into each bowl to cover the noodles, adding a few chrysanthemum leaves and mushrooms. Garnish with ginger, and sprinkle lightly with sesame seeds and togarashi, if desired.

# UDON WITH JAPANESE PORK AND VEGETABLE CURRY

**Serves 6**

2 tablespoons butter or vegetable oil

1 small yellow onion, chopped

1 tablespoon freshly grated ginger

1 large garlic clove, grated

1 tablespoon Indian curry powder

2 tablespoons all-purpose flour

4 cups *Kombu Dashi* (kelp stock, page 51)

2 tablespoons thin soy sauce

2 tablespoons honey or apple sauce

1½ pounds boneless pork country ribs, cut into 1-inch chunks

9 baby Red Bliss potatoes, halved

4 large carrots, peeled and sliced ½ inch thick

4 ounces green beans, halved crosswise

10 ounces cremini mushrooms, halved

1 pound fresh or 10 to 12 ounces dried udon

2 scallions, trimmed and thinly sliced on the diagonal

Thick udon noodles are a perfect match for a mildly spicy and yellow curry sauce. Pork, potatoes, cremini mushrooms, carrots, and green beans make for a colorful and healthful dish. The Japanese have been eating curries since the nineteenth century, when the British introduced them to Indian curry. Japanese curries are eaten with rice, udon, or bread, with pork as the preferred meat. Unlike their spicy Indian cousins, Japanese curries are mild, and they contain the salty-sweet combination of honey or grated apple and soy sauce. If you ask a Japanese home cook how to make Japanese curry, he or she will often tell you to buy instant Japanese curry roux and bouillon cubes. That's the "authentic" way of making Japanese curry, and it can be delicious! I make it here from scratch as a way to share with you my understanding of how this unique curry is created. You can also try the ground pork, sirloin beef, or ramen noodle variations below.

In a large pot, melt the butter or heat the oil over medium heat and sauté the onion until golden, 5 to 7 minutes. Add the ginger and garlic and sauté until fragrant, about 1 minute. Add the curry powder and flour and whisk vigorously for 1 minute. Add the stock, 1 cup at a time, whisking to incorporate it with the roux smoothly. Add the soy sauce and honey and stir. Reduce the heat to medium-low, add the pork and potatoes, and cook, covered, for 20 minutes. Add the carrots, green beans, and mushrooms, and continue to cook, covered, until the the meat is cooked through, the vegetables are tender, and the sauce is slightly thickened, 25 to 30 minutes more.

Meanwhile, bring a pot of water to a boil over high heat, and cook the noodles until tender yet firm, about 10 seconds for fresh udon, or 5 minutes for dried. Drain and divide among large soup bowls or plates. Ladle the curry over the noodles, including some of each ingredient in each serving. Garnish with the scallions.

## Variations

Substitute 1 to 1½ pounds of coarsely ground pork for the country ribs. Add it after stir-frying the garlic and ginger, but before adding the curry powder and flour, and proceed with the recipe.

Use 1½ pounds of sirloin steak, cut into chunks, instead of the pork. Stir-fry it in a lightly oiled pan over high heat until medium-rare and set aside. Add the beef to the curry just minutes before serving it.

Substitute ramen for the udon. If precooked, heat in boiling water for 10 seconds, and if dried, boil for 3 minutes.

# UDON SOUP WITH SPICY CABBAGE, SHIITAKES, AND PORK TENDERLOIN

**Serves 6**

In Korea, thick wheat noodles similar to Japanese udon are enjoyed in broths along with preserved spicy cabbage, known as kimchi. Other popular ingredients may include shiitake mushrooms, beef, pork, or seafood. This type of soup is so popular that packages of instant spicy udon with kimchi are available. Kimchi can be purchased in Korean or Japanese markets, and sometimes in health food stores. Choose one that has been made with Napa cabbage or a combination of Napa cabbage and daikon. The soup stock should be as plain as possible because the kimchi and shiitakes will provide the flavor. This soup is also delicious made with thin, curly ramen.

2   quarts *Kombu Dashi* (kelp stock, page 51) or Basic Asian Stock (pork, page 46)

2   cups kimchi

8   dried shiitake mushrooms, soaked in water until pliable, stemmed, and caps quartered

2   ounces fresh ginger, sliced

2   scallions, trimmed and cut into 1-inch pieces

1   teaspoon dark sesame oil

Kosher salt and freshly ground black pepper to taste

1   pound fresh or 12 ounces dried udon

12   ounces pork tenderloin, thinly sliced against the grain

Toasted sesame seeds for garnish

In a medium pot, heat the stock over medium-low heat. Add the kimchi, mushrooms, ginger, scallions, and sesame oil. Adjust the seasoning with salt and pepper. Reduce the heat to low and simmer, covered, until ready to serve.

Bring a medium pot of water to a boil and cook the noodles until tender yet firm, about 5 minutes for dried udon and 10 seconds for fresh. With a strainer, transfer and divide the noodles among large soup bowls. Using the same cooking water, cook the pork until opaque, about 1 minute. Drain and divide the pork among the servings of noodles. Ladle 1 or more cups of broth with kimchi and shiitakes over each portion of noodles and serve garnished with sesame seeds.

# PINK PLUM-FLAVORED NOODLES WITH SPINACH AND MUSHROOMS

**Serves 6**

Flavored noodles are popular in Japan, where green tea and pink plum are used to color and deepen the flavor of buckwheat or wheat noodles (pages 96 and 57, respectively). I like to use the thin Japanese pink plum somen here, creating a cold dish with spinach and cremini mushrooms, also known as baby portobellos. Complemented with a sweet, savory, and tangy dressing, the recipe makes a wonderful light lunch or a refreshing dinner on a warm day. If you can't get the pink somen, use the regular kind.

¼  cup thin soy sauce

2  tablespoons mirin

2  tablespoons rice vinegar

1  tablespoon honey

¼  cup vegetable oil

2  teaspoons dark sesame oil

1  teaspoon freshly grated ginger

1  scallion, trimmed and thinly sliced

1  pound baby spinach

1  pound cremini or shiitake mushrooms

8  ounces dried pink plum somen

Freshly ground black pepper

Toasted sesame seeds for garnish

In a large salad bowl, whisk together the soy sauce, mirin, rice vinegar, honey, 1 tablespoon of the vegetable oil, the sesame oil, ginger, and scallion. Set the dressing aside.

In a large skillet or wok, heat 1 tablespoon of the oil over high heat and stir-fry half the spinach until just wilted, 1 to 2 minutes. Transfer to a plate. Repeat with the remaining spinach. To the same skillet add 1 more tablespoon of oil and stir-fry the mushrooms until tender, about 5 minutes. Add to the spinach and set aside.

Bring water to a boil in a medium pot, and cook the noodles until tender yet firm, about 2 minutes. Drain and shock in iced water. Drain again thoroughly and add to the dressing. Drain the spinach and mushrooms completely and add to the mix. Season with pepper to taste, toss well, and divide among large individual bowls or plates. Serve garnished with sesame seeds.

# EGG NOODLES

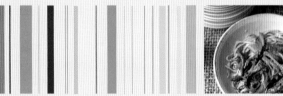

**CHAPTER 5**

# EGG NOODLE TYPES

## CHINESE EGG NOODLES

**DAN MIAN:** These are sold as fresh Chinese egg noodles, but they are precooked and can be reheated for 10 seconds if serving in broth, or added directly to stir-fries. Thick and round, they are sold in 1-pound bags.

**LA MIAN:** A Chinese ramen, which is very similar to Japanese ramen (see below). It is always sold dried in stacks of 8 to 10 square cakes, which are individual servings, but without any seasoning packets. Chinese dried ramen tend to be slightly thinner than the Japanese type. Cook these for about 3 minutes.

**MIAN BAO:** These flat egg noodles are slightly wider than Italian linguine, but thinner. They are available fresh or dried. The fresh are raw, not precooked, and are sold in 1-pound bags. Cook for about 10 seconds. The dried noodles are formed into portion-size round nests and sold with about eight in a package. Cook for about 3 minutes.

**MIAN XIAN:** This long egg noodle is similar to angel hair pasta, but thinner and more brittle. The egg note is fairly pronounced here because the noodles are made with salted eggs rather than fresh ones. Cook for about 2 minutes.

**SHIAZI MIAN:** These very thin shrimp- or crab-flavored noodles are sold dried, and are often formed into individual portion–size round cakes resembling bird's nests. They are sold in packages of eight. These cook in about 2 minutes and should be loosened with chopsticks as they are boiling.

**SHI DAN MIAN:** These fresh egg noodles are raw (not precooked), thin, and curly. Sold in 1-pound bags, they almost feel dry to the touch, but they are very pliable. Cook for about 2 minutes

**YOU MIAN (DRIED):** These dried egg noodles are sold in packages of about eight individual portion-size nests. They are thinner than fresh *you mian* and resemble angel hair pasta. Cook for about 2 minutes. Although the Chinese word for these noodles, *you mian,* is spelled like the word for its dried counterpart (below), the difference is all in the accent and tone. But that's a different book!

**YOU MIAN (FRESH):** These fresh egg noodles are oily and are sold raw or precooked in 1-pound bags. They are slightly thicker than spaghetti and can be added directly to stir-fries or boiled for 10 seconds before serving in broth.

## JAPANESE AND KOREAN EGG NOODLES

**RAMEN (DRIED):** Dried ramen is packaged in individual portions with seasoning packets included for an instant meal. It cooks in about 3 minutes.

**RAMEN (FRESH):** Sometimes referred to in Japanese as *chuka soba,* meaning "Chinese noodle," fresh ramen is usually not precooked. It is sold packaged in individual square cakes with seasoning packets similar to those that come with dried ramen. Like the dried, it is an instant noodle. Reheat for 10 seconds in boiling water, or add directly to stir-fries.

**RAMYEON (DRIED):** This Korean ramen is sold in instant noodle packages like the Japanese version. In addition to the plain version, *ramyeon* comes in many interesting flavors, including kimchi, seafood, and beef. It cooks in about 3 minutes. The noodles are often stir-fried and served with an egg on top. The egg can be added raw and mixed into the noodles while they are still piping hot, or the egg can be cooked over easy or sunny-side up.

You have probably eaten Asian egg noodles without thinking about it. They appear in many familiar dishes, ranging from the crispy fried noodle strips that accompany Chinese-American sweet and sour soup, to Szechuan cold sesame noodles, to Japanese ramen.

You may also have eaten noodles that you thought were egg noodles because they had a beige to yellow color. These may have been egg- and wheat-based with food coloring added to intensify the color. Or they may have been the so-called yellow noodles—noodle dough with an alkaline mineral water added as a substitute for eggs. This mineral water colors and firms up the dough, creating light yellow noodles that are particularly chewy.

Chinese egg and yellow noodles are extremely popular in snack items throughout the country, either plain or flavored with shrimp or crab. They are available fresh, precooked, or dried. The dried are usually sold in single-portion-size clumps resembling nests. The fresh noodles are normally loosely gathered into plastic bags and sold by weight.

The egg noodles come in a wide variety of shapes and sizes—long or short, thick or thin, round or flat. In essence, the most popular Chinese egg noodles echo the patterns found in wheat noodles: they are similar in shape to the familiar Italian capellini (angel hair), vermicelli, spaghettini, spaghetti, linguine, and fettuccini. Some specialty noodles exist. The two most popular are the large, square, thick egg wrappers used for making egg rolls, and small, round or square, thin wrappers for making dumplings. (See Chapter 9 for more information on dumplings and rolls.)

The Japanese also make wide use of egg noodles. Ironically, perhaps the best-known and most widely available egg variety in Japan—the delicate ramen—is Chinese in origin. It is believed that the word *ramen* is derived from the names of several Chinese noodles, including *lao mian* ("old noodles") and *la mian* ("hand-pulled noodles"). These noodles first became very popular throughout Japan in the mid- to late-nineteenth century, when the Japanese also

began adding pork, beef, and chicken to their traditional fish and rice cuisine. These proteins and ramen seemed a beautiful marriage, eventually spawning regional variations served in ramen noodle shops across the land. Ramen can be thick or thin, curly or straight. It may be flavored with miso, or served in a milky pork broth. There are hundreds of traditional ways to enjoy ramen.

Instant ramen are one of my quick meal favorites, a trick I learned from my mother as a child. Mom served instant ramen noodles in broth to my brothers and me as a snack when we came home from school in the afternoon or after we played in the winter snow. The noodles warmed us up and made us smile. (We also liked slurping the broth.) I still enjoy instant ramen—delicate, slightly chewy noodles in a bowl of steaming broth. I add snow peas, romaine lettuce leaves, or anything green to the gently boiling broth. I slice leftover roast chicken as a quick add-on, too. It makes for a balanced meal—starch, protein, and vegetables—in minutes.

In general, then, I like the versatility and richness of Asian egg noodles. They are great stir-fried, especially with beef and broccoli, and equally delicious served in soup with squid, shrimp, and scallops. I cook them shaped into a cake as wide as the pan, and fry the cake until golden on both sides to create a base for a juicy seafood stir-fry. Another favorite are thin egg noodles and wontons served in a light broth flavored with sesame oil and scallions. It's a sort of egg noodle soup, and it's great comfort food. Although I prefer my egg noodle dishes hot, noodle salads served at room temperature are also tasty. These are some of my husband's favorite dishes. My daughter likes all kinds, as long as she gets to slurp.

## SOME TIPS AND GUIDELINES

Balance is a key concept when cooking Asian noodles. And while there are no hard and fast rules, try to use them as the Italians use their pasta. For example, choose a thin egg noodle (similar to vermicelli) for vegetarian noodle dishes, a thick round noodle (slightly thicker than spaghetti) to complement meat stir-fries, and perhaps something in the middle like flat egg noodles (similar to small linguine) for seafood.

When serving a thick noodle with seafood or meat, add some vegetables to balance out the protein and starch. Thin noodle dishes can also be adjusted. If you are serving a delicate noodle, such as somen, with protein and vegetables, add some broth to lighten the dish. That way, the delicate noodles are not overwhelmed.

Having noted all of this, ramen is the best all-purpose, most readily available egg noodle. It is neither too light nor too heavy for most dishes—a perfect workhorse that complements just about any protein and vegetable.

Fresh or precooked egg and yellow noodles can be found in the refrigerated section of specialty markets. They should be kept refrigerated and consumed within 2 days of purchase. Dried egg and yellow noodles can be kept in a dark cool place and should be consumed within 6 months. Fresh egg noodles are slightly chewy; dry noodles tend to be less so.

# EGG NOODLES WITH WONTON SOUP AND ASIAN GREENS

Serves 6

I've always enjoyed wontons, tiny morsels of ground pork and shrimp meticulously folded into an egg noodle wrapper and set afloat in a fragrant chicken or pork broth, flavored with dark sesame oil. A generous sip (actually, a slurp!) of broth follows each delightful bite. The addition of thin, round egg noodles and Asian leafy greens such as bok choy or *choy sum* extends the experience.

2 quarts Basic Asian Stock (pork or chicken, page 46)

1 pound fresh or 8 to 10 ounces dried ramen, or 12 ounces fresh thin Chinese egg noodles

1 recipe of Pork and Shrimp Wontons (page 147)

2 teaspoons dark sesame oil

4 cups leafy greens, such as baby bok choy or *choy sum*

Kosher salt and freshly cracked black pepper

2 scallions, trimmed and thinly sliced

Chili-garlic sauce for serving (optional)

In a medium pot, bring the stock to a boil over high heat. Reduce the heat to low, cover, and simmer until ready to serve.

Bring a large pot of water to a boil over high heat and cook the noodles until tender yet firm, about 3 minutes for dried ramen, 10 seconds for fresh ramen, and about 2 minutes for fresh Chinese noodles. Use a strainer to fish out the noodles and drain. Divide the noodles among large soup bowls.

Return the water to a boil, add the wontons, and cook, allowing them to surface to the top, about 5 minutes. Drain and divide the wontons among each serving of noodles.

Add the sesame oil and leafy greens to the stock, adjust the seasoning with salt and pepper to taste, and cook for 1 minute. Ladle a generous amount of stock over each serving of noodles and wontons, making sure to divide the greens evenly. Garnish with scallions and serve with chili-garlic sauce (if using) on the side for dipping the wontons.

# EGG NOODLE SOUP WITH FIVE-SPICE DUCK

**Serves 6**

2 tablespoons thin soy sauce

2 tablespoons sugar

1 ounce ginger, finely grated

1 large garlic clove, finely grated

1 teaspoon five-spice powder

1 tablespoon vegetable oil

6 boneless duck magrets, about
10 ounces each, skin side
scored in criss-cross pattern

2 quarts Basic Asian Stock
(chicken, page 46)

1½ pounds daikon, peeled, halved,
and sliced crosswise ½ inch
thick

1 pound fresh or dried thin egg
noodles

Fried Scallions in Oil (page 40) or
Fried Garlic in Oil (page 39) for
drizzling

1 bunch fresh cilantro, stems
trimmed, for the broth

Egg noodle soup tends to be hearty for the simple reason that Asian egg noodles are heavy in egg flavor and content. For this reason I prefer to eat these noodles in the winter, when cold temperatures seem to call for rich foods. This recipe is a bit out of the ordinary and is likely to be the topic of conversation if you're having guests. The noodles are boiled and drizzled with fragrant and colorful scallion oil. Pan-fried and sliced five-spice duck breast, rich with licorice flavor, is set atop. The broth, with its sliced daikon, is served on the side for sipping, a common ritual at Asian tables. You can follow my basic Asian stock recipe, but if you feel so inclined, use meaty duck bones instead of chicken.

Duck breast is sold in halves and is often labeled "magrets." The magrets are from ducks that have been fattened to produced foie gras. A magret weighs about 10 ounces; a third of that weight is the thick fat layer and skin. To render the fat while cooking, be sure to score the skin about ⅛ inch deep. You can also remove the fat entirely, but the crispy fat is extraordinarily delicious.

In a large bowl, whisk together the soy sauce and sugar until the sugar is completely dissolved. Add the ginger, garlic, five-spice powder, and oil and continue to whisk until well combined. Add the duck breasts and rub all over with the marinade. Marinate for 30 minutes at room temperature or 1 hour in the refrigerator.

Bring the stock to a boil over medium heat. Reduce heat to low and simmer, covered, until ready to serve. About 10 minutes before serving, add the daikon to the pot and cook until tender.

Heat a large skillet over medium heat. Add the duck breast, skin side down, and cook until golden crisp, 3 to 5 minutes. Turn the duck skin side up and cook until medium-rare, 5 to 7 minutes, or to desired doneness.

Meanwhile, bring a large pot of water to a boil over high heat. Add the egg noodles and cook until tender yet firm, about 2 minutes for fresh, 10 seconds for precooked, and 3 minutes for dried. Drain and divide among large soup bowls or plates.

Slice the duck thinly against the grain and set the equivalent of one breast on top of each serving of noodles. Drizzle generously with the scallions in oil. Place a generous amount of cilantro sprigs into individual rice bowls, and ladle some of the broth with daikon in each one. Serve alongside the noodles, and replenish as necessary.

# RAMEN IN BROTH WITH TEMPURA VEGETABLES AND IMITATION CRAB STICKS

**Serves 6**

Japanese soups are typically light, with not an ounce of fat in the broth, which is generally seaweed–based and is flavored with soy sauce, sake, and mirin. Here the ramen is complemented by fresh vegetable tempura and imitation crab sticks (made of pulverized white fish), available in Japanese or Korean markets. Tempura, introduced by the Portuguese over 600 years ago, is easy to make at home. The batter can be used to deep-fry all sorts of vegetables and herbs. I am particularly fond of tempura made with root vegetables. In this dish the orange sweet potatoes, green asparagus spears, and purple Asian eggplant add color to the soup. If you can find fresh green or purple shiso leaves—popular in Japanese and Korean cooking—be sure to add them to your tempura. They are delicious battered and deep–fried, and offer a floral yet mustardy note to the dish.

Peanut oil for deep-frying

2   large eggs

¼   cup chilled sake or light beer

1   cup ice water

1¼ cups all-purpose flour

2   quarts Primary or Secondary Dashi (page 51)

2   tablespoons thin soy sauce

2   tablespoons mirin

1   teaspoon dark sesame oil

1   pound fresh or 8 to 10 ounces dried ramen

2   small to medium orange sweet potatoes, sliced ¼ inch thick on the diagonal

1   bunch green asparagus, woody ends snapped or cut off

2   Asian eggplants, sliced ¼ inch thick on the diagonal

Fill a medium pot halfway up with peanut oil and heat to 360°F to 375°F.

In a medium to large bowl, lightly beat the eggs with the sake or beer and water. Add the flour all at once, giving it a few stirs. Do not whisk because the batter should remain lumpy. Refrigerate until ready to use.

In a medium pot, bring the dashi to a gentle boil over medium-low heat. Reduce the heat to low, add the soy sauce, mirin, and sesame oil, simmer, covered, until ready to use.

Bring a large pot of water to a boil over high heat. Cook the ramen until tender yet firm, about 3 minutes for dried, 10 seconds for fresh. Drain, and divide among large soup bowls.

12 fresh green or purple shiso
   leaves (optional)

6 imitation crabsticks, halved
  crosswise

2 scallions, trimmed and chopped

2 ounces ginger, finely julienned

Toasted sesame seeds for
   garnish

Togarashi pepper or cayenne
   pepper (optional)

Dry the sweet potatoes, asparagus, eggplant, and shiso (if using) thoroughly. Working in small batches so as not to cool the oil, dip the vegetables in the batter and deep-fry until golden on all sides, about 3 minutes per batch. Drain on a paper towel–lined plate.

Ladle about 1¼ cups of stock over each serving of ramen, and top with pieces of crabsticks and vegetable tempura. Or serve the vegetables on the side to keep them crispy. Garnish the noodle soup with scallions, ginger, and sesame seeds. Sprinkle lightly with togarashi, if desired.

# STIR-FRIED EGG NOODLES WITH BEEF AND BROCCOLI

**Serves 6**

Egg noodles with beef and broccoli is a Chinatown restaurant classic, made with either Chinese or Western broccoli, depending on the cook's preference. Fresh round egg noodles about the size of spaghetti are used here. Although they are called fresh, the thick egg noodles known as *dan mian* (literally "egg noodle") are precooked and do not need to be boiled for this recipe. Seasoned with soy sauce, oyster sauce, and Shaoxing wine (Chinese rice wine), this hearty dish is perfect for winter. If you cannot find fresh *dan mian*, feel free to use the dried version of this noodle or thinner fresh or dried ramen. If you use ramen, you might want to cut the beef into strips to balance the textures.

- **3** tablespoons thin soy sauce
- **3** tablespoons oyster sauce
- **3** tablespoons Shaoxing wine or sake
- **1** tablespoon sugar
- **1** tablespoon tapioca starch or cornstarch
- **1** teaspoon dark sesame oil
- **1** pound beef sirloin, thinly sliced
- **1** pound fresh or 10 ounces dried thick round egg noodles, or 1 pound fresh or 10 ounces dried ramen
- **2** tablespoons vegetable oil
- **3** large garlic cloves, crushed and finely chopped
- **1¼** cups Basic Asian Stock (chicken, page 46)
- **1** pound Chinese broccoli or common broccoli, cut into bite-size chunks or florets

**Freshly ground black pepper**

In a medium bowl, whisk together 1 tablespoon each soy sauce, oyster sauce, and rice wine. Add the sugar and continue to whisk until completely dissolved. Stir in the tapioca starch and continue stirring until smooth. Add the sesame oil and beef, and mix well. Marinate for 20 minutes.

If using dried Chinese egg noodles or ramen, bring a large pot of water to a boil over high heat and cook the noodles until tender yet firm and drain.

Heat 1 tablespoon of the vegetable oil in a skillet or wok over high heat and stir-fry the garlic until fragrant, about 10 seconds. Add the beef and stir-fry until tender, 1 to 2 minutes. Transfer to a plate. Add the remaining tablespoon of oil with ¼ cup of the stock and cook the broccoli until tender, 3 to 5 minutes. Transfer the broccoli to the same plate.

Add the remaining cup of stock and the remaining 2 tablespoons each of soy sauce, oyster sauce, and rice wine to the same skillet and bring to a boil over high heat. Add the noodles and cook until the liquid has almost completely evaporated, leaving the noodles lightly moistened, 2 to 3 minutes. Return the beef and broccoli to the skillet and toss to mix the ingredients thoroughly. Season with pepper to taste and serve.

# SWEET AND SPICY BREAKFAST EGG NOODLES WITH FRIED EGG AND HERBED CHICKEN

**Serves 6**

I love breakfast noodles. One of my most memorable experiences eating stir-fried egg noodles was in Indonesia, where I was visiting my aunt. The noodle dish, called *mee goreng*, was topped with a sunny-side-up egg and crispy chicken wings, all boldly seasoned with herbs and spices. My version is simple, recalling the original, but using readily available ingredients. Try this with an egg cooked your favorite way and pan-grilled chicken, a healthier alternative to deep-fried wings. The dish is a perfect recipe to try on the weekends, when you may have more time to devote to cooking a balanced meal in the morning. Be sure to moisten your bamboo skewers and to choose ones that will fit perfectly in your grill pan.

2   tablespoons fish sauce

2   tablespoons sugar

2   lemongrass stalks, trimmed to 8 to 10 inches and grated (see page 23)

1   small shallot, minced

1   large garlic clove, finely grated

2   red Thai chilies, stemmed, seeded, and minced (see Note)

1   pound boneless skinless chicken, thinly sliced

10   ounces fresh thin Chinese egg noodles, or 1 pound fresh or 8 ounces dried ramen

In a medium bowl, stir together the fish sauce and sugar until the sugar is completely dissolved. Stir in the lemongrass, shallot, garlic, and chilies. Add the chicken and mix well. Thread the chicken on the bamboo skewers, place on a plate, and cover with plastic wrap. Marinate at room temperature for up to 30 minutes or in the refrigerator for up to 1 hour.

Bring a large pot of water to a boil over high heat. Cook the noodles until tender yet firm, about 2 minutes for fresh Chinese egg noodles, 3 minutes for dried ramen, and 10 seconds for fresh ramen. Drain, shock under cold running water, and drain again.

Heat an oiled grill pan over medium-high heat. Brush some oil over the skewered chicken and grill until cooked through and golden, about 2 minutes per side.

2 tablespoons vegetable oil, plus extra for brushing the chicken

¼ small green cabbage, cut into ¼-inch-wide strips

2 tablespoons thin soy sauce

Kosher salt and freshly cracked black pepper

6 large eggs

12 medium bamboo skewers, soaked in water for about 20 minutes

Meanwhile, in a large skillet, heat the 2 tablespoons of oil over high heat and stir-fry the cabbage until tender and caramelized, about 7 minutes. Add the noodles, season with the soy sauce, and adjust the seasoning with salt and pepper to taste, as necessary. Toss well and cook until heated through, about 3 minutes. Divide the noodles among 6 large individual plates and place 2 chicken skewers alongside each serving.

In a well-greased skillet over medium to high heat, cook the eggs, any style, and place one on top of each noodle serving.

**NOTE:** You can substitute 1 to 2 teaspoons chili-garlic sauce for the fresh Thai chilies.

# STIR-FRIED EGG NOODLES WITH PORK, CABBAGE, AND SHIITAKE MUSHROOMS

**Serves 6**

My mother often stir–fried egg noodles, shiitake mushrooms, green cabbage, and pork. It was a simple and tasty dish, seasoned lightly with soy sauce and black pepper. We ate it for dinner and had leftovers the next day when we came home from school. Mom has always liked fatty cuts of meat like pork butt or country rib. She said they were sweeter and made the food taste better. (With a hint of guilty pleasure in mind, I agree.) This recipe makes me a bit nostalgic; it's a throwback to the bad old days when Asian ingredients were just about absent from Western markets. My mom would struggle to get it right, using green cabbage instead of Napa cabbage and spaghetti instead of Asian noodles. These days she usually uses Napa cabbage and fresh ramen, which is actually precooked. If you want to use lean pork, choose pork tenderloin for a more healthful version of the dish.

- 1 pound fresh or 12 ounces dried ramen

- 3 tablespoons vegetable oil

- 1 large garlic clove, minced

- 12 dried shiitake mushrooms, soaked in water until pliable, stemmed, and caps julienned

- 1 pound pork butt, boneless country rib, or tenderloin, thinly sliced or julienned

- ¼ small green cabbage, cut into ¼-inch strips

- ¼ cup thin soy sauce

- 1 teaspoon dark sesame oil

- Freshly cracked black pepper

- Garlic-chili sauce for serving (optional)

Bring a medium pot of water to a boil and cook the noodles until tender yet firm, about 10 seconds for the fresh ramen and 3 minutes for the dried. Drain the noodles.

In a large nonstick skillet, heat 1 tablespoon of the oil over medium-high heat. Stir-fry the garlic until fragrant, about 1 minute. Add the mushrooms and stir-fry until just crispy, about 2 minutes, and transfer to a plate. Replenish the wok with 1 teaspoon of the oil, and stir-fry the pork until cooked, about 5 minutes. Add the cabbage and return the mushrooms to the wok. Season with 2 tablespoons of the soy sauce, toss, and stir-fry until the cabbage is tender, about 7 minutes. Add the noodles, the remaining vegetable oil and soy sauce, and the sesame oil. Toss to distribute the ingredients evenly throughout and season with pepper to taste. Divide among large bowls or plates and serve with chili-garlic sauce on the side, if you wish.

# COLD SESAME EGG NOODLES

**Serves 6**

This cold sesame noodle dish is one of the most popular dishes in Chinese restaurants. My family recipe is simple, made with readily available ingredients. It's a great blank canvas for adding all sorts of leftover proteins. I have made the dish with shredded roast chicken and duck, as well as sliced pork and beef. Sesame paste, often referred to as tahini, can be found in health food stores or the international foods aisle of your supermarket. If you can't find it, try unsalted 100 percent pure peanut or almond butter, which will give you different, but equally tasty, results.

1   pound fresh thin Chinese egg noodles, or 10 ounces fresh or dried ramen

¼   cup rice vinegar

3   tablespoons sesame paste, almond butter, or peanut butter

3   tablespoons soy sauce

2   tablespoons honey

1   tablespoon dark sesame oil

1   teaspoon or more chili-garlic sauce

2   scallions, trimmed and thinly sliced

6   sprigs fresh cilantro, stems trimmed

Bring a large pot of water to a boil over high heat. Cook the noodles until tender yet firm, about 2 minutes for fresh Chinese noodles, 10 seconds for fresh ramen, and 3 minutes for dried ramen. Drain the noodles and shock in ice-cold water. Drain again.

In a large bowl whisk together the vinegar, sesame paste, soy sauce, honey, sesame oil, and chili-garlic sauce until smooth. Add the noodles and toss well to distribute the sauce evenly throughout. Garnish with the scallions and cilantro and serve at room temperature or slightly chilled.

# WONTON STRIPS WITH SPICY CRAB AND BACON STIR-FRY

**Serves 6**

Square dumpling wrappers are not just for making dumplings. They can also be cut into short, 1/4- to 1/2-inch-wide strips and cooked with delicious results. This spicy crab-and-bacon stir-fry combination was given to me by an Indonesian friend living in New England. Indonesians love hot, spicy foods, and this dish is no exception. Feel free to add the fresh chilies to your taste. I do not use oil for this stir-fry. The bacon usually has enough fat for stir-frying the other ingredients.

1  pound fresh square dumpling wrappers, cut into 1/4- to 1/2-inch-wide strips or 1 pound fresh broad rice noodles

1 to 2 tablespoons vegetable oil

8  ounces sliced bacon

1  large garlic clove, minced

1  large shallot, minced

2  scallions, trimmed and minced

2  lemongrass stalks, trimmed to 8 to 10 inches and grated (see page 23)

3 to 4 red Thai chilies, stemmed, seeded, and minced

12 to 16 ounces lump crabmeat

1  cup fresh shelled green peas, or frozen peas, thawed

Fish sauce

Freshly ground black pepper

Bring a medium pot of water to a boil over high heat. Cook the dumpling-wrapper noodles until tender yet firm, about 1 minute. Drain, toss with the oil, and divide among individual soup bowls or plates.

In a wok or large skillet over high heat, stir-fry the bacon until it renders its fat and is crispy, 3 to 5 minutes. Add the garlic, shallot, scallions, lemongrass, and chilies, and continue to stir-fry until golden, about 5 minutes. Add the crabmeat and peas and toss well. Season with the fish sauce and pepper to taste and divide among the servings of noodles. Serve hot.

# TWICE-COOKED EGG NOODLE CAKE WITH BRAISED SEAFOOD

**Serves 6**

This classic fried—egg noodle pancake is called *liang mien hwang* in Chinese, which literally means "two sides brown." It is topped with a braised seafood mixture flavored with fresh ginger, scallion, soy sauce, and sesame oil. The velvety sauce soaks into the crispy noodles, moistening them without compromising their crisp texture. I love to combine rings of calamari with small shrimp and tiny bay scallops for a combination of tender and chewy textures. The sliced carrots and snow peas add color and crunch. Any vegetable and seafood or meat combination will make a great topping for these crispy noodles, so feel free to experiment. Be sure to make enough sauce to keep the noodles moist, but not so much that they will become soggy.

12 ounces fresh curly Chinese egg noodles, or 1 pound fresh or 8 to 10 ounces dried ramen

3 tablespoons vegetable oil

2 large garlic cloves, minced

1 ounce ginger, finely julienned

2 scallions, trimmed and cut into 1-inch pieces

18 medium headless tiger shrimp, shelled and deveined

12 baby squid, tentacles separated, cleaned, and cut into ½-inch rings

18 medium scallops

1 cup snow peas, ribs removed

1 medium carrot, peeled and sliced on the diagonal

1 cup Basic Asian Stock (chicken, page 46) or Chinese Superior Stock (page 47)

1 tablespoon thin soy sauce

2 teaspoons tapioca starch or cornstarch

1 tablespoon dark sesame oil

Kosher salt and freshly ground black pepper

Bring a large pot of water to a boil over high heat. Cook the noodles until tender yet firm, about 2 minutes for fresh Chinese egg noodles, 10 seconds for fresh ramen, or 3 minutes for dried ramen. Drain. Take an 8-inch plate, put the noodles on top, and shape them into a round cake the size of the plate.

In a 9- to 10-inch nonstick skillet, heat 1 tablespoon of the oil over medium heat. Slide the round cake of noodles into the pan and cook until golden and crisp, about 5 minutes. Place a plate over the skillet and carefully invert the noodles onto the plate (use oven mitts to avoid burning your hands). Add another tablespoon of the oil to the skillet and slide the noodles, soft side down, back into the skillet to crisp, about 5 minutes more. Slide the crispy cake onto a serving plate.

Heat the remaining tablespoon of oil in a wok or large skillet over high heat. Stir-fry the garlic, ginger, and scallions until fragrant, about 1 minute. Add the shrimp, squid, and scallops and continue to stir-fry until cooked through, about 3 minutes. Add the snow peas and carrots. In a bowl whisk together the stock, soy sauce, and tapioca and stir into the seafood and vegetable stir-fry. Add the sesame oil, and season with salt and pepper to taste. Keep stir-frying until the sauce is slightly thickened. Ladle the seafood and sauce over the center of the crispy noodle cake and serve hot.

**Variation**

To transform this dish into an elegant appetizer, cook 6 individual crispy noodle cakes in a small nonstick skillet following the instructions, and top each with some of the seafood and sauce.

# SHRIMP-FLAVORED NOODLES WITH SHRIMP AND SNOW PEAS

**Serves 6**

Flavored Chinese noodles are a delicious alternative to plain egg noodles. Thinner than angel hair pasta, these delicate noodles are best served in a light broth. The crunchy snow peas provide a nice counterpoint to the delicate noodles and slightly chewy shrimp. The Fried Garlic in Oil complements the soup perfectly, giving it a sweet, garlicky finish. One teaspoon is just about perfect for each steaming bowl of noodles.

If you cannot find shrimp-flavored noodles, use another thin dried Asian egg noodle. You can also try making the soup with crunchy, leafy pea shoots instead of snow peas, blanching these the same way.

2 quarts Basic Asian Stock (chicken, page 46)

1 ounce ginger, finely julienned

2 scallions, trimmed and cut into 1-inch pieces

2 teaspoons sesame oil

12 ounces dried shrimp-flavored noodles

2 cups snow peas, ribs removed

1 pound small headless tiger shrimp, peeled and deveined

Kosher salt and freshly ground black pepper

Fried Garlic in Oil (page 39)

In a medium pot, bring the stock to a gentle boil over medium heat. Reduce the heat to low, add the ginger, scallions, and sesame oil, and simmer, covered, until ready to serve.

Bring a large pot of water to a boil. Cook the noodles until just firm, about 1 minute. Using a strainer, fish out the noodles, drain, and divide among large soup bowls. In the same cooking water, blanch the snow peas until just tender, about 30 seconds. With a slotted spoon, remove the snow peas and divide them among the bowls of noodles. Add the shrimp to the cooking water and cook until opaque, about 1 minute. Drain and divide the shrimp equally among the bowls. Adjust with salt and pepper to taste and garnish with the Fried Garlic in Oil.

# CRAB-FLAVORED NOODLES WITH VELVETY CRAB SAUCE AND GREEN PEAS

**Serves 6**

Crab sauce with green peas is a classic combination. I've had it served over rice in some of New York City's best Chinese restaurants, and I offer it here in a noodle variation. The delicate crab sauce is lightly thickened with tapioca starch, seasoned with salt and pepper, and visually enhanced with egg white, which makes the sauce look like a fluffy cloud. The green peas and the tiny red flying fish roe garnish add color to the otherwise white canvas.

Crab-flavored noodles are sold dried in bundles resembling nests. If you cannot find them, use another thin dried Asian egg noodle. Flying fish roe can be found in Japanese, Korean, or gourmet supermarkets.

Bring a large pot of water to a boil over high heat.

Meanwhile, in a large skillet or wok, heat the oil over high heat. Stir-fry the garlic and ginger until fragrant, about 1 minute. Add the stock, lower the heat to medium-low, and add the egg whites, gently swirling them about to create long strands. Add the crabmeat and peas. Mix the tapioca with 2 tablespoons of water and add to the sauce, stirring to distribute evenly and prevent gummy lumps. Add the sesame oil and let the sauce thicken slightly. Adjust the seasoning with salt and pepper to taste.

Bring a pot of water to a boil. Cook the noodles until tender yet firm, 1 to 2 minutes, and drain. Divide among large individual bowls or plates and top each serving with an equal amount of crab sauce and green peas. Garnish with some of the flying fish roe (if using) and a sprig or two of cilantro.

## Ingredients

- 2 tablespoons vegetable oil
- 1 large garlic clove, minced
- 1 ounce ginger, freshly grated
- 2 cups Basic Asian Stock (chicken, page 46)
- 2 large egg whites, lightly beaten
- 1 pound lump crabmeat, crumbled
- 1 cup fresh shelled green peas, or frozen peas, thawed
- 1 tablespoon tapioca starch or cornstarch
- 1 teaspoon dark sesame oil
- Kosher salt and freshly ground black pepper
- 12 ounces crab-flavored dried noodle nests
- 2 tablespoons flying fish roe (optional)
- 8 to 12 fresh cilantro sprigs (leaves only)

# BUCKWHEAT NOODLES

CHAPTER **6**

Buckwheat noodles, widely known as soba, are popular in Japanese cuisine. They are wholesome and slightly chewy in texture, and are eaten hot, at room temperature, or cold. Made with a combination of wheat and buckwheat flour, they are a specialty of northern Japan. Light beige when fresh and dark brown when dried, these long, thin noodles come square or round. They are good tossed with a soy sauce and sesame oil salad dressing or served in a hot broth with all sorts of shredded meats, seafood, and vegetables.

Soba is readily available in supermarkets and health food stores, where it is sold dried. In New York City and other urban areas (and increasingly in suburban and rural health food stores) cold soba dishes are available as a ready-to-go lunch.

Soba has more texture and flavor than most noodles. It's nutty and wholesome like whole-grain breads. It can be subtly grainy when made fresh from stone-ground buckwheat flour. I like stir-fried soba so much that when I go to my local Japanese restaurant, I order *yaki soba* (stir-fried egg noodles) and ask them to substitute the buckwheat black soba noodles for the eggy yellow ones. I don't have to ask anymore because when they see me walk in the door, they say "stir-fried black noodle, right?" I grin and nod yes, anticipating the wonderful steaming dish complete with chicken, broccoli florets, bamboo shoots, and baby corn. Definitely home-style in spirit, it is tasty seasoned ever so lightly with soy sauce and sesame oil.

I also enjoy cooking green tea soba, called *cha soba* in Japanese. Dark green, with a distinctly bitter green tea flavor, these noodles are prepared in all the ways that you would cook regular soba. They are worth discovering; I especially like these as a cold noodle dish tossed with wild mushrooms in a light sweet-and-savory mirin and soy sauce dressing. At my country home in Upstate New York, black trumpets and oyster mushrooms grow wild on the forest floor. They lend fragrance, texture, and style to a dish with their different shapes and colors. The earthy recipe presented on page 103 captures the colors and scents of autumn, when these wild mushrooms are in season.

When cooking with Japanese buckwheat noodles, the idea is to keep the flavors subtle. For one, it is in keeping with the Japanese approach to cooking. In addition, you want the flavor of the noodle, not the accompanying ingredients, to come to the fore. "Pure" and "clean flavors" are the words that should be foremost in your mind when cooking soba; this applies to the green tea version as well as regular soba.

Buckwheat noodles are available fresh (not precooked), frozen, or dried. The fresh and frozen noodles can be purchased in Japanese and Korean markets, in addition to the dried. The dried noodles are sold in packages of three to ten individually wrapped portions, with a ribbon twined around each portion. Look for these in the international foods aisle of your supermarket or in the local health food store. Whether fresh or dried, they should be cooked in boiling water before you add them to stir-fries or serve them in broth. If you can get your hands on fresh noodles, do try them as they offer a very different texture than the dried version. Both are delicious, just different.

Frozen soba should be kept frozen until you are ready to use them. Keep the fresh noodles refrigerated and consume them within 2 days. The dried noodles will keep in a dry, dark, and cool place and should be eaten within 6 months. Feel free to use regular or green tea soba interchangeably in the recipes that follow.

# SOBA IN BROTH WITH GARLAND CHRYSANTHEMUM LEAVES

**Serves 6**

While any leafy green will make for a delicious soba noodle soup, it is worth your while to find fresh garland chrysanthemum leaves, which are usually sold in Japanese and Chinese markets. The floral taste of these slender leaves (called *shingiku* in Japanese and *tong ho* in Chinese) is extraordinary and knows no substitute. Edible chrysanthemum comes in a variety of shapes and colors, from light to dark green. If you decide to grow your own chrysanthemums, be sure to buy seeds specifically labeled as edible types. This recipe also calls for white miso, a soybean paste that is actually tan in color and is sold smooth or grainy in texture. Buy the smooth type. Although the miso is readily available in Asian markets or health food stores, you can use thin soy sauce in a pinch for a different but complementary flavor.

2½ quarts *Kombu Dashi* (kelp stock, page 51)

⅓ cup thin soy sauce or white miso paste

¼ cup sake

¼ cup mirin

12 dried shiitake mushrooms, soaked in water until pliable, stemmed, and caps julienned

10 to 12 ounces soba noodles

1 tablespoon dark sesame oil

1 pound leafy greens, such as chrysanthemum, baby bok choy, or spinach

2 scallions, trimmed and thinly sliced into rounds

2 ounces ginger, finely julienned

Toasted sesame seeds for garnish

Togarashi pepper to taste (optional)

In a large pot, combine the stock, soy sauce or miso (if using miso, dilute it in a little of the stock), sake, and mirin. Add the mushrooms, cover, and bring to a gentle boil over medium heat. Reduce heat to low and continue to simmer until ready to use.

Meanwhile, bring a medium pot of water to a boil over high heat and cook the noodles until tender yet firm, about 3 minutes. Drain and divide among large soup bowls.

Add the sesame oil and leafy greens to the soup stock and cook for 30 seconds. Ladle a generous amount of stock with greens and mushrooms over each serving of noodles. Garnish with scallions, ginger, and sesame seeds. Add a sprinkle or two of togarashi, if desired.

# CLASSIC COLD SOBA WITH FRIED PORK CHOP

**Serves 6**

Known as *zaru soba* in Japan, this cold buckwheat noodle specialty is ethereal. Boiled then shocked in chilled spring water, the noodles are traditionally left to drain on a bamboo mat set over a deep square plate, which collects any remaining water. Garnished with shredded nori, a seaweed sold in paper-thin square sheets, the cold noodles are eaten dipped in a light dashi-based sauce flavored with wasabi, daikon, and scallion. Sipping the leftover sauce, diluted with the hot cooking water from the noodles, makes for a wonderful palate-cleansing ritual. Simple yet complex in flavor, *zaru soba* is a perfect summer noodle dish, especially if you want to give a sense of ritual and sophistication to your table and create a special memory for your guests.

Soba easily complements many different foods. Here I combine the chilled noodles with another Japanese classic called *tonkatsu*, a deep-fried pork chop, for a heartier meal. The thin boneless pork chops are breaded with panko, which are coarse Japanese breadcrumbs. For an elegant presentation, serve the noodles and meat with a side of salad greens. Nori and panko are available in health food stores, large supermarkets, and gourmet food shops.

2 cups *Kombu Dashi* (kelp stock, page 51)

¾ cup thin soy sauce

¾ cup mirin

1½ tablespoons sugar

2 tablespoons wasabi powder

4 ounces daikon, peeled and finely grated

2 scallions, trimmed and minced

8 to 10 ounces dried soba or green tea soba noodles

6 cups chilled spring water

1 large sheet nori, cut into thin strips

Bring the dashi, soy sauce, mirin, and sugar to a gentle boil over medium heat. Remove from the heat and allow to cool.

In a small bowl stir the wasabi powder with 1 tablespoon water. Mix well and roll the paste between the palms of your hands, until fully combined and a ball forms. (Your hands should come clean as you work the paste, a sign that the consistency is just right.) Divide equally among 6 plates (about 1 teaspoon for each). Place a small mound of daikon and scallions on each plate. Cover loosely with plastic wrap (so as not to disturb the mounds).

Bring a large pot of water to a boil over high heat and add the soba noodles. Return the water to a boil and cook the noodles until tender but firm, about 3 minutes. Meanwhile, pour the chilled spring water into a large bowl. Reserving the cooking water, use a strainer to pick up the noodles and transfer to the chilled spring water. Drain the noodles. Divide them equally among 6 individual plates and sprinkle some nori over each serving. Pour the dipping sauce into individual little bowls. Serve the noodles with the fresh garnishes and dipping sauce on the side.

To eat, stir some daikon, wasabi, and scallion into the dipping sauce. Take some noodles with your chopsticks and dip them. Optionally, when you have finished eating the noodles, pour some of the hot noodle cooking water into the remaining dipping sauce and sip just as you would tea.

**Vegetable oil for deep-frying**

1   cup all-purpose flour

6   boneless pork chops,
    ¼ inch thick

2   large eggs, beaten

2   cups panko

**Kosher salt and freshly ground
    black pepper**

6   cups baby salad greens, such as
    mesclun

**Pickled ginger (optional)**

To serve the noodles with fried pork chop and salad greens: Heat a medium pot filled a third of the way with oil to 360°F to 375°F over medium heat.

In a resealable plastic bag combine the flour and the pork chops. Seal the bag and toss to coat each chop evenly all over.

Put the eggs in a shallow bowl and scatter the panko on a plate. Dip each pork chop in the egg wash, then cover completely with panko. Deep-fry the meat in batches until golden and crispy all over, about 2 minutes total. Drain on a paper towel–lined plate. Sprinkle with salt and pepper to taste. Cool for 15 minutes, then cut each chop into ¼-inch-thick diagonal slices.

To serve, divide the baby salad greens equally among shallow bowls and top with noodles. In a bowl, stir the dashi with daikon, scallions, and wasabi to taste, and drizzle generously over the noodles. Add a sliced pork chop to each serving and garnish with pickled ginger, if using.

**NOTE:** To make your own panko, take an unsliced loaf of white bread (Pullman, country bread, or baguette, for example), cut away the crust, and dry it thoroughly for 24 hours at room temperature. Then, use the medium side of a box grater to grate the loaf.

# SOBA AND SEAFOOD SOUP

**Serves 6**

Use your favorite seafood to make this simple buckwheat noodle and seafood soup. While I like to use shrimp, squid, and small bay scallops for their chewy textures, you can just as successfully use a white-fleshed fish such as flounder, sea bass, or catfish, and crab or lobster will work, too. Fresh scallions and ginger complement the seafood and add a delicious and pungent note to the finish.

2 quarts Japanese Kelp Stock (any type, page 51)

¼ cup thin soy sauce

¼ cup sake

¼ cup mirin

10 ounces dried soba noodles

16 medium to large tiger shrimp, heads removed, peeled and deveined

4 medium squid, cleaned and cut into ½-inch rings

1 cup bay scallops, drained

1 tablespoon dark sesame oil

8 Napa cabbage leaves, cut into 1-inch pieces

2 scallions, trimmed and thinly sliced

2 ounces ginger, finely julienned

Toasted sesame seeds for garnish

Togarashi pepper (optional)

In a medium pot, combine the kelp stock, soy sauce, sake, and mirin. Cover and bring to a gentle boil over medium to low heat. Reduce the heat and simmer until ready to use.

Meanwhile, bring a large pot of water to a boil over high heat. Cook the noodles until tender yet firm, about 3 minutes. Use a strainer to scoop out the noodles and divide them among large soup bowls. Add the shrimp and squid to the same cooking water and cook until opaque, about 30 seconds. Add the scallops and cook for an additional 30 seconds. Drain and divide the seafood among the servings of noodles.

Add the sesame oil and Napa cabbage to the soup stock and cook for about 2 minutes. Ladle a generous amount of stock with cabbage over each serving of noodles, and garnish with scallions, ginger, and sesame seeds. Add a sprinkle or two of togarashi, if desired.

# STIR-FRIED SOBA WITH FISH CAKE, VEGETABLES, AND CHICKEN

**Serves 6**

This stir-fried soba recipe is a family favorite, which we like with chicken, broccoli, carrots, and onions added to the mix. This is a quick meal to assemble; I sometimes add Japanese fish cake, which can be found in Japanese or Korean markets. Accompanied by a side of miso soup or light broth, this noodle stir-fry makes for a hearty lunch.

¼ cup thin soy sauce

2 tablespoons mirin

1 tablespoon tapioca starch or cornstarch

1 tablespoon dark sesame oil

1 ounce ginger, finely grated

1 scallion, trimmed and minced

8 to 10 ounces boneless skinless chicken breast

8 ounces dried soba noodles

¼ cup vegetable oil

1 small red or yellow onion, cut into thin wedges

2 cups small broccoli florets

1 medium carrot, peeled and cut into matchsticks

¼ cup julienned fish cake

Freshly ground black pepper

In a medium bowl, stir together 2 tablespoons of the soy sauce, the mirin, and tapioca starch until smooth. Stir in the sesame oil, ginger, and scallion. Add the chicken and mix thoroughly. Set aside to marinate the chicken for 20 minutes.

Bring a large pot of water to a boil over high heat. Cook the noodles until tender yet firm, about 3 minutes. Drain, shock under cold running water, and drain again.

Heat 1 tablespoon of the oil in a large skillet over high heat. Stir-fry the onion until translucent, 3 to 5 minutes, add the broccoli and carrot, and continue to stir-fry until just tender, about 3 to 5 minutes. Transfer to a plate. Add another tablespoon of the oil to the same skillet. Add the chicken and stir-fry, separating the slices, until cooked through, 3 to 5 minutes. Transfer to the plate with the vegetables. Add the remaining 2 tablespoons of oil and stir-fry the soba noodles with the remaining 2 tablespoons of soy sauce until heated through, about 5 minutes. Return the vegetables and chicken to the skillet and continue to stir-fry for a few seconds to mix thoroughly. Divide among large plates, garnish with fish cake, and sprinkle with black pepper, if desired.

# SOBA WITH BEEF AND WATERCRESS

**Serves 6**

Beef and peppery watercress is a flavor combination that holds up to the hearty character of soba noodles. Here the tender beef is marinated in the basic Japanese seasonings of soy sauce, sake, and sesame oil before it is stir-fried with the watercress. I like tender cuts of beef, and in the colder months, I sometimes like them fatty, too. For a relatively low-fat version of this dish, use beef filet mignon. If you like buttery cuts, choose hanger steak or rib steak. Or use your favorite cut of beef, pork, or even chicken.

2 tablespoons thin soy sauce

2 tablespoons mirin

1 tablespoon sugar

2 teaspoons dark sesame oil

1 tablespoon tapioca starch or cornstarch

1 ounce ginger, finely grated

1 scallion, trimmed and minced

Freshly ground black pepper

1 pound beef, such as filet mignon, hanger steak, or rib steak, thinly sliced against the grain

10 ounces dried soba noodles

2 tablespoons vegetable oil

2 to 3 bunches watercress, stems trimmed

Toasted sesame seeds for garnish

In a medium bowl, stir together the soy sauce, mirin, and sugar until the sugar is completely dissolved. Stir in the sesame oil, tapioca starch, ginger, and scallion, and season with pepper to taste. Add the beef, tossing it well to coat the slices evenly throughout. Let stand for 20 minutes at room temperature or for up to 1 hour, refrigerated.

Bring a large pot of water to a boil and cook the noodles until tender yet firm, about 3 minutes. Drain and divide among large plates.

Heat 1 tablespoon of the oil in a large skillet or wok over high heat and stir-fry the beef until medium to medium rare, 2 to 3 minutes. Divide among the noodle servings. Add the remaining oil and stir-fry the watercress until just wilted, about 2 minutes. Put an equal amount atop each serving of noodles, and garnish with toasted sesame seeds.

# COLD GREEN TEA SOBA WITH WILD MUSHROOMS AND SPINACH

**Serves 6**

This vegetarian dish made with cold green tea soba can be served as a full meal, or as a perfect accompaniment to any grilled or roasted meats or seafood. Fresh shiitakes are called for here, but rehydrated dried shiitakes will do, though their flavor is beefier. I like to combine the shiitakes with wild mushrooms such as chanterelles, black trumpets, and oyster mushrooms. If you cannot find these, look for other types of wild or exotic mushrooms or increase the quantity of the shiitakes.

10 ounces dried green tea soba noodles

3 tablespoons vegetable oil

1 large garlic clove

8 fresh shiitake mushrooms, stemmed, and caps julienned

8 large oyster mushroom, halved or quartered

12 chanterelle mushrooms

12 black trumpet mushrooms, halved or quartered

1 pound baby spinach

3 tablespoons thin soy sauce

3 tablespoons rice vinegar

3 tablespoons mirin

1 teaspoon wasabi powder

2 teaspoons dark sesame oil

Freshly ground black pepper

1 scallion, trimmed and minced

⅓ cup pickled ginger, drained

Toasted sesame seeds for garnish

Bring a large pot of water to a boil over high heat. Cook the noodles until tender yet firm, about 3 minutes. Drain, shock under cold running water, and drain again. Transfer to a mixing bowl.

In a medium to large skillet, heat 1 tablespoon of the oil over high heat and stir-fry the garlic until fragrant and golden, about 30 seconds. Add the shiitakes, oyster mushrooms, chanterelles, and black trumpets and stir-fry until just wilted, 1 to 2 minutes. Add the mushrooms and garlic to the noodles. In the same skillet heat 1 tablespoon of the oil and stir-fry the spinach until just wilted, about 1 minute. Transfer to the noodles and toss to mix the ingredients well.

In a small bowl, whisk together the soy sauce, vinegar, mirin, wasabi, remaining tablespoon of vegetable oil, and sesame oil until smooth. Pour over the noodles, and season with pepper to taste. Toss well and divide the noodles among individual large pasta bowls. Garnish each serving with some scallion, pickled ginger, and toasted sesame seeds.

# GREEN TEA SOBA AND SMOKED WILD SALMON ROLLS

**Makes 12 rolls**

Think sushi roll when making this fun dish, which can be served as an appetizer or a light lunch. The soba noodles, smoked wild salmon, and fresh sprouts (such as clover, lentil, or pea) are rolled in nori (dried seaweed), making for a surprisingly wonderful combination of flavors and textures. Like sushi rolls, these soba rolls are cut into bite-sized pieces and dipped into soy sauce spiked with wasabi. Serve with pickled ginger on the side for the full effect.

4   ounces dried green tea
    soba noodles

12  sheets nori

8   ounces smoked wild salmon,
    skin removed, meat crumbled

2   cups fresh sprouts or micro
    greens, such as mizuna, tatsoi,
    or baby spinach

Thin soy sauce for serving

Wasabi paste for serving

Pickled ginger for serving

Bring a medium pot of water to a boil over high heat. Cook the noodles until tender yet firm, 3 to 5 minutes. Drain and shock under cold running water. Drain again. Immediately separate the noodles into 12 portions, straightening them out almost as they were in the package.

Wrap a sushi mat with plastic and place it in front of you. Put a nori sheet directly on top of the mat and add one portion of noodles, stretching it across the width of the sheet, and leaving 1 inch of nori on the edge farthest from you clear of noodles. Scatter some salmon on top of the noodles, beginning about 1 inch from the edge of the nori closest to you. Top with sprouts. Roll the noodles and nori over the filling, enclosing the ingredients fairly tightly. Repeat until you have a total of 12 rolls. They should be about the size of large cigars.

With a very sharp knife, trim the ends if necessary, then cut each roll into 8 equal pieces. Serve with soy sauce, wasabi, and pickled ginger on the side.

# SOBA WITH GRILLED ASPARAGUS AND SEA SCALLOPS WITH SWEET MISO SAUCE

**Serves 6**

In this dish the soba is flavored with Fried Scallions in Oil and topped with grilled asparagus and sea scallops glazed with a sweet miso sauce. During the summer you can grill the asparagus outdoors. The smoky flavor of a wood charcoal fire adds complexity to this substantial meal. While I call for green asparagus, try making the dish with a colorful array of asparagus—green, white, and purple. White miso, which is called *shiro-miso* in Japanese, can be found in health food stores. Smooth rather than grainy miso is preferable for this recipe.

3 tablespoons sugar

¼ cup sake

3 tablespoons mirin

2 tablespoons rice vinegar

⅓ cup white miso

1 tablespoon finely grated ginger

¼ cup vegetable oil

10 ounces dried soba noodles

36 medium asparagus spears, woody ends snapped or cut off

18 sea scallops

Kosher salt and freshly ground black pepper

12 walnut halves, lightly toasted (see Note) and coarsely chopped

In a bowl, whisk together the sugar, sake, mirin, and rice vinegar until the sugar is completely dissolved. Add the white miso, ginger, and 1 tablespoon of the oil and whisk until well combined. Set the miso glaze aside.

Bring a large pot of water to a boil over high heat and cook the noodles until tender yet firm, about 3 minutes. Drain, shock under cold running water, and drain again.

Heat a well-oiled grill pan over medium heat. Brush the asparagus and scallops with all or most of the remaining 3 tablespoons of oil and season with salt and pepper to taste. Grill the asparagus first until just tender, 3 to 5 minutes total, rolling them about to heat them evenly all around. Divide and top each noodle serving with asparagus. Grill the scallops in the same pan until cooked through and crisp on each side, about 2 minutes per side. Divide the scallops among the servings of noodles, and spoon some miso glaze over each. Serve garnished with toasted walnuts.

**NOTE:** To toast the walnut halves, put them in a dry skillet over medium-low heat for about 3 minutes, being sure to shake the pan so as not to burn the pieces. Remove from the pan and cool slightly before chopping.

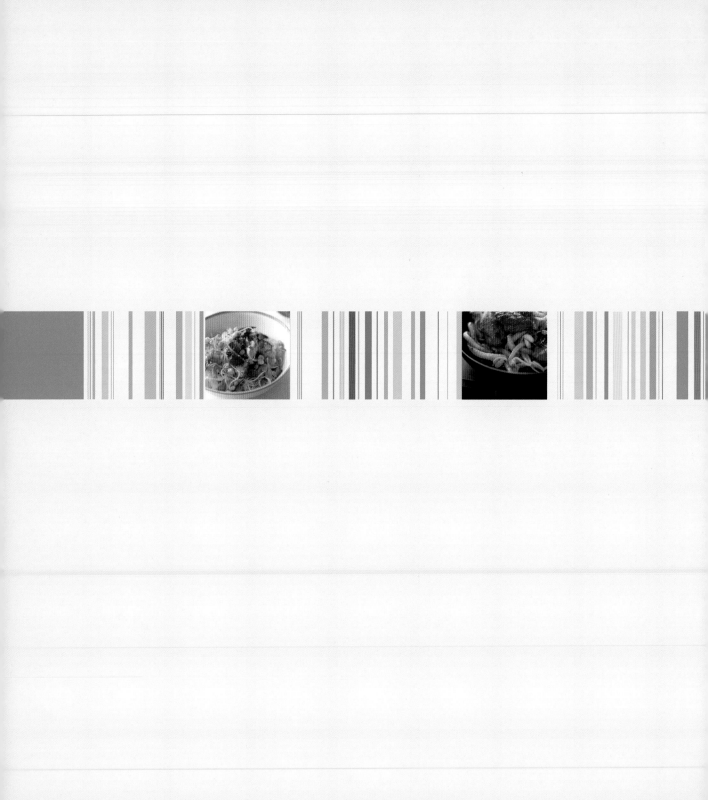

# RICE NOODLES

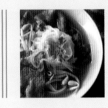

CHAPTER **7**

One of my fondest memories is the rice noodle soup we enjoyed almost every weekend when I was a kid. We would have one of two versions, *pho bo* (page 121), which is also called simply *pho*, and *kway'teo* (page 113). *Pho* is a specialty from northern Vietnam. It is a sort of Vietnamese fast food—not because it is not nutritious (it is), but because *pho* is found everywhere. It is available in shops on just about every corner throughout Vietnam, and in the streets, where *pho* peddlers balance freshly made rice noodles on one end of their bamboo poles while balancing the broth, condiments, and stacks of bowls and chopsticks on the other. *Pho* is a wonderful concoction of sweet anise-scented broth, slightly chewy rice noodles, all sorts of refreshing herbs, and protein. Beef (*pho bo*) is traditional, while chicken (*pho ga*) and seafood (*pho do bien*) are contemporary variations. Spicy chili-garlic sauce and sweet hoisin sauce always accompany the soup for dipping the beef.

There are as many versions of *kway'teo* as there are Southeast Asian home cooks. The *kway'teo* I recall most vividly was handed down from my Chinese grandmother Huong to my mother, after her marriage to my father. My grandmother was born in Canton, a southern province in China. But the family had migrated to Phnom Penh, in southern Cambodia in the 1930s, and eventually to Saigon (renamed Ho Chi Minh City), Vietnam. The south seemed to be in the family's blood, and with it came a devotion to the southern habit of eating egg- and rice-based noodle dishes. I love my family's *kway'teo*, which is sweet and smoky at the same time. The broth is made

# RICE NOODLE TYPES

## CHINESE RICE NOODLES

**HE FEN:** This flat broad rice noodle sheet is sold fresh (technically, it is precooked). Oily and pliable, it can be sliced to any thickness. A popular classic made with these is called *sha he fen* (page 123). The sheet is also used to make *ha cheung*, a Cantonese dim sum shrimp roll specialty (page 161). These cook in about 5 minutes when steamed as a wrapper or stir-fried.

**MI FEN:** These are dried thin rice vermicelli, which are often served in broth. They are also used for making the classic Singapore Noodles (page 117). They cook in about 10 seconds.

**NEN DZEM FEN:** These fresh (precooked) noodles are short and thick and are hand-rolled into 2- to 3-inch-long pieces that are tapered at each end. (Think of a super-thick, flexible toothpick!) These are known as silver pins. They cook in about 5 minutes.

## VIETNAMESE NOODLES

**BANH HOI:** These dried vermicelli are used in soups and often are simply boiled and topped with all sorts of fresh vegetables and a grilled protein. These will cook in about 5 seconds.

**BANH PHO:** These dried flat rice sticks come in small, medium, and large sizes. The medium ones resemble thin linguine, while the large ones look like fettuccini. The smallest noodles are thin and narrow. They cook very quickly, in about 10 to 15 seconds, depending on the size.

**BUN:** These fresh (precooked) round noodles are often served with fresh vegetables and grilled proteins. In a pinch, you can use *banh hoi* (see above). Reheat these in boiling water for a couple of seconds.

with meaty pork bones, ground pork, and dried shrimp (or dried squid), and the rice noodles are always cooked until just tender. The best part of the soup is the garnish of chopped cilantro, fresh red Thai chilies, fried garlic oil, and preserved Tien Sin cabbage. I could eat this part-Chinese, part-Cambodian, and part-Vietnamese soup every day. Like wontons (page 147), it is comfort food to me.

My *Indochine* preferences aside, the Chinese have many excellent classic dishes made with rice noodles. Two—*sha he fen* and *ha cheung*—are absolute standouts. Both are made with fresh broad rice noodle sheets. For s*ha he fen,* the noodles are thickly sliced and stir-fried with tender beef slices, stained delicately with soy sauce. It must be cooked in a super hot wok, and the trick is to use plenty of oil so the noodles don't stick together like glue. In Chinese restaurant kitchens these noodles fly high as the chef deftly gives the wok a few jerks with his wrist. The wrist action is such an important part of stir-frying that there is a specific word for it: *Pao!* (If you have a strong wrist, go for it.)

*Ha cheung* (page 161) is the dim sum specialty my husband will do handstands for. The rice noodle sheets are cut into 3-inch squares, which are filled with shrimp, rolled up, and steamed. It can be had in restaurants, of course, but I make this at home as a family style plate. It sits piled up high on a large serving dish, steaming hot and redolent with just-made rice noodles and absolutely fresh shrimp. (We make forays to Chinatown for the noodles on the morning they will be cooked.) Born of basic ingredients and accented with humble dipping sauces, it is nonetheless an unforgettable experience when made this way.

I would be remiss if I did not point out two more classics: Singapore Noodles (page 117) and pad Thai (page 125). Singapore noodles are a favorite on Chinese-American restaurant menus. Lightly seasoned with Indian curry powder (hence "Singapore ") and stir-fried with leftover Cantonese roast pork, shrimp, and peas, they are made with delicate, thin vermicelli–style rice noodles.

Pad Thai is another immensely popular stir-fried noodle dish. At once sweet, sour, and savory, the dish is enjoyed in Thai restaurants throughout the world as well as at the renowned midnight bazaars of Chiang Mai and Bangkok, in Thailand. Celebrated as a national dish, it can be prepared with shrimp, chicken, or pork, and I give instructions for all these variations here.

## NOTES ON RICE NOODLES

Rice is the most important starch in the Asian diet, except in China's most northern regions (where wheat is historically dominant). In China, Japan, Korea, the Philippines, Thailand, Vietnam, Cambodia, Laos, Indonesia, Malaysia, and India, for example, rice has always been regarded as the main dish, and everything else—including meats, seafood, and vegetables—are accompaniments. In China when the cook calls you to the table, he or she says *"chi fen,"* which literally means "eat rice"—simply an expression for "let's eat." Rice is predominantly eaten as a boiled grain, to be sure, but rice noodles are very much part of the Asian diet as well.

Like other Asian noodles, rice noodles come fresh or dried, though the fresh noodles are actually precooked, not raw. Rice noodles come in a wide variety of shapes: long or short, round or flat, thin or thick, and as precooked broad sheets or dried papers (see Chapter 9: Buns, Dumplings, and Spring Rolls). Depending on where they are made—China and Thailand are the largest exporters of rice noodles—the dried versions will have different textures. Some are made with rice flour, water, and salt. Others are made with sticky rice flour, while still others contain tapioca starch or cornstarch to give the noodle a more springy texture. Dried rice noodles are available in health food stores or the international food aisles of your supermarket.

Fresh (precooked) broad rice noodle sheets can be cut up into thin or thick strips and added to broths, stir-fries, and other dishes. As noted previously, they can also be cut into squares and rolled around shrimp stuffing (page 161). Once refrigerated, however, the noodle hardens and is useless for making the rolls. They can still be added directly to soups or stir-fries, however; as soon as they hit the hot surface of your cooking vessel, they soften perfectly.

## SOME TIPS AND GUIDELINES

All fresh noodles are found at noodle shops in Chinatown or in the refrigerated section of specialty markets. They should be kept refrigerated and consumed within 2 days of purchase, with the exception of freshly made broad noodles that you intend to stuff. Those you must buy the day you will prepare them, and keep them out of the refrigerator. Dried noodles can be stored for up to 1 year, although I generally like to consume them within 6 months. Fresh or dried, rice noodles (also called rice sticks) are generally sold in 1-pound bags.

Before cooking with dried rice noodles, soak them in water (room temperature or cold) for about 20 to 30 minutes, until pliable. Never use hot water to soften dried rice sticks: it softens them too much, preventing them from cooking evenly when stir-fried or served in soups.

When serving rice noodles in a broth, soak them and then boil them in water for a few seconds. Do not add the noodles directly to the broth. Once boiled, nestle them in a soup bowl and ladle the broth on top. These steps will ensure that your broth remains clear and presentable.

# RICE NOODLE SOUP WITH GROUND PORK AND SHRIMP

**Serves 6**

My family's *kway'teo* recipe is one I will pass along to my daughter. It is the dish I crave when I'm tired and feeling under the weather. Although the original recipe calls for dried shrimp to flavor the stock, fish sauce will do quite nicely. But in that case, add fresh shrimp to your soup. Cilantro stems are edible, just like the leaves, and in my family we use the herb in all its parts. (The stems are not very fibrous and hold a great deal of flavor.) Preserved Tien Sin cabbage can only be found in Asian markets. There is no real substitute for this ingredient, but if you cannot find it, the soup will still be delicious.

8 to 10 ounces dried narrow flat rice sticks, soaked until pliable

24 small headless tiger shrimp, shelled and deveined (optional)

2 cups mung bean sprouts

2½ quarts Southeast Asian Stock (page 48) or Basic Asian Stock (pork, page 46)

1 pound coarsely ground pork

⅓ cup small dried shrimp (optional)

Fish sauce

Freshly ground black pepper

3 limes, quartered

1 cup chopped fresh cilantro

3 scallions, trimmed and thinly sliced

Fried Garlic in Oil (page 39) for serving

6 fresh red Thai chilies, stemmed, seeded, and sliced

Chili-Garlic Sauce (see page 21) for serving

Preserved Tien Sin cabbage (optional) for serving

Bring a large pot of water to a boil over high heat and cook the noodles until tender yet firm, about 10 seconds. Use a strainer to scoop out and drain the noodles, and to divide them among large soup bowls. If using, cook the fresh shrimp in the same water until opaque, about 1 minute. Drain, and distribute the shrimp among the servings of noodles. Top each one with some mung bean sprouts.

In a large pot, bring the stock to a boil over high heat. Working in batches, put some ground pork in a ladle, adding some hot broth to it. With a fork or spoon stir the pork to loosen it, and release it into the pot. Repeat with the remaining pork. Add the dried shrimp, if using, or season with fish sauce and pepper to taste, and continue to boil for about 5 minutes.

Ladle the broth, along with some pork and dried shrimp (if using) into each bowl, making sure to cover the noodles and bean sprouts. Taking a lime wedge or two, squeeze fresh lime juice into each bowl, and garnish each serving with fresh cilantro, scallions, fried garlic in oil, some chili slices, chili-garlic sauce, and Tien Sin cabbage (if using).

# RICE NOODLES WITH FRIED FISH, HERBS, AND PEANUTS

**Serves 6**

This dish of *bun* (fresh rice noodles) with fried fish and stir-fried herbs is a specialty of Hanoi. Bite-size morsels of fish are dredged in rice flour (and turmeric for color) so they don't fall apart when fried. The fried fish are surprisingly light. Although the inclusion of dill surprises people, it is widely used in Vietnamese cuisine. This dish will give you a sense of how generously fresh herbs are often used in Vietnamese cooking. They are very much a part of the meal, rather than a garnish, and are equal in importance to the fish and noodles. If you cannot find fresh *bun*, use rice vermicelli instead.

1   pound fresh *bun*, or 10 ounces dried rice vermicelli

Vegetable oil for deep-frying, plus 1 tablespoon for stir-frying

1   cup rice flour or all-purpose flour

1   teaspoon ground turmeric

Kosher salt and freshly ground black pepper

2   pounds skinless white fish fillets, such as catfish or flounder, cut into bite-size chunks

4   scallions, trimmed, halved lengthwise, and cut into 1-inch-long pieces

⅓   cup unsalted dry-roasted peanut halves

1   bunch fresh Thai basil (leaves only)

1   bunch fresh cilantro, stems trimmed

1   bunch fresh dill, stems trimmed

Sweet, Sour, and Spicy Fish Sauce (page 41)

Bring a large pot filled with water to a boil over high heat and cook the *bun* for about 10 seconds. (If using dried vermicelli, soak the noodles until pliable, about 30 minutes, and boil until tender yet firm, about 10 seconds.) Drain and divide the noodles among large individual bowls.

Pour enough oil into a medium pot or wok to come a third of the way up the sides and heat to 360°F to 375°F over medium heat.

Meanwhile, put the flour and turmeric into a resealable plastic bag and sprinkle lightly with salt and pepper. Add the fish. Seal the bag and shake until the pieces are well coated. Working in 6 batches, deep-fry the fish until golden and crisp on all sides, about 2 to 3 minutes total per batch. Drain on a paper towel–lined plate and divide among the servings of noodles.

While deep-frying, heat 1 tablespoon of oil in a skillet over high heat and stir-fry the scallions until wilted. Add the peanuts, basil, cilantro, and dill and continue to stir-fry until fragrant and wilted, about 30 seconds more. Arrange a generous amount of stir-fried herbs over each serving of noodles and fish and serve with the fish sauce on the side. Each guest should drizzle 2 tablespoons of the sauce (or more to taste) over his or her serving to loosen the noodles and season the overall dish.

# SINGAPORE NOODLES

**Serves 6**

Singapore-style noodles are a favorite in Chinese-American restaurants and are traditionally made using leftover Cantonese roast pork. The dish is lightly seasoned with Indian curry powder, giving the thin rice noodles a beautiful yellow hue. The curry flavor explains the dish's name: Singapore cooking exhibits a significant Indian influence. Stir-fried with small shrimp and peas, this colorful dish can be made ahead of time and very successfully reheated.

Cantonese roast pork can be found in Chinese markets. You'll recognize the long and thick reddish-golden meat strips hanging in the window to entice passersby.

8  ounces dried rice vermicelli, soaked in water until pliable

24  small tiger shrimp, heads removed, peeled and deveined

3  tablespoons vegetable oil

1  small onion, cut into thin wedges

½  cup fresh shelled green peas, or frozen peas, thawed

2  teaspoons Indian curry powder

6  ounces Cantonese roast pork or thick slice of ham, diced

1½ tablespoons fish sauce

Kosher salt and freshly ground black pepper

6  sprigs cilantro, trimmed

Bring a pot of water to a boil over high heat and cook the noodles until tender yet firm, about 10 seconds. Use a strainer and tongs to pick up the noodles and transfer them to a bowl. In the same water cook the shrimp until opaque, about 1 minute, and drain.

Heat 1 tablespoon of the oil in a large skillet or wok over high heat. Stir-fry the onion until golden, 3 to 5 minutes. Add the remaining 2 tablespoons of oil, the noodles, and peas, and sprinkle the curry powder over the top. Toss well, making sure all of the noodles become yellow. Add the pork, shrimp, and fish sauce, and continue to stir-fry until the noodles are heated through, about 5 minutes. Adjust the seasoning with salt and pepper, if necessary, and serve garnished with cilantro.

# SPICY COCONUT RICE NOODLES AND CHICKEN SOUP

**Serves 6**

Adapted from *kao soi*, a traditional northern Thai coconut curry noodle soup, this recipe uses Thai curry paste and Indian curry powder as a flavor base. Rich with herbs and spices, it is sweet, spicy, salty, sour, and bitter all in the same mouthful. Lemongrass, now readily available, also plays a big role in this fragrant soup, lending it a wonderful citrus note. Although coconut milk is rich, here it is mixed with Asian chicken stock to produce a relatively light broth. In Chiang Mai, arguably the culinary capital of northern Thailand, the soup is served with rice noodles or egg noodles. Feel free to experiment: ramen are wonderful in the soup, for example. The fish sauce is essential for seasoning this Southeast Asian–inspired soup. Finally, be sure to shake the cans of coconut milk before opening so as to completely blend the cream and liquid.

2  tablespoons vegetable oil

1  large garlic clove, minced

1  shallot, minced

4  lemongrass stalks, trimmed to 8 to 10 inches and grated (see page 23)

1½ to 2 tablespoons Thai red curry paste

1  tablespoon Indian curry powder

¼  cup palm sugar or light brown sugar

2  tablespoons fish sauce

5  cups unsweetened coconut milk

4  cups Basic Asian Stock (chicken, page 46)

Juice of 2 limes

Salt and freshly ground black pepper

Heat the oil in a large pot over medium heat, and stir-fry the garlic, shallot, and lemongrass until golden, about 5 minutes. Add the curry paste and powder and continue to stir-fry for 1 minute. Add the sugar and fish sauce, and continue to stir-fry until slightly caramelized, about 2 minutes. Add the coconut milk, stock, and lime juice. Adjust the seasoning with salt and pepper to taste. Reduce the heat to low and simmer, covered, for 1 hour.

Bring a large pot of water to a boil over high heat and cook the noodles until tender yet firm, about 10 seconds. Drain and divide among large soup bowls. Top each serving with some snow peas and mung bean sprouts.

8   ounces dried narrow flat rice
    sticks, soaked in water until
    pliable

2   cups snow peas, boiled for 1 or
    2 minutes

2   cups mung bean sprouts

6   boneless skinless chicken
    thighs, thinly sliced

12  sprigs fresh cilantro

Bring the flavored broth to a gentle boil over medium heat. Add the chicken, stir, and boil gently until cooked through, about 5 minutes. Ladle a generous amount of the broth with sliced chicken over each serving of noodles. Serve garnished with cilantro sprigs.

# RICE NOODLE SOUP WITH BEEF AND HERBS

**Serves 6**

This is the national dish of Vietnam. Originating from the northern city of Hanoi, *pho bo,* as it is called in Vietnamese (or simply *pho*), is a rice noodle and beef soup with a fragrant, sweet beef broth flavored with star anise, cloves, and cinnamon. Variations of this dish are made with chicken or seafood (see below). All are delicious. If the broth is made ahead of time, the soup requires little effort for spectacular results. Use flat dried rice sticks for this soup. Also, freeze the block of beef for 30 to 45 minutes so you can slice it evenly into paper-thin slices. The beef cooks in the bowl of piping hot broth, but you can blanch the slices of meat before adding them to your bowl of soup if you prefer not to have raw beef at the table.

8 to 12 ounces dried narrow flat rice sticks, soaked in water until pliable

2½ quarts Vietnamese Beef Stock (page 49)

1 small yellow onion, thinly sliced

Fish sauce or salt

2 cups mung bean sprouts

1 to 1½ pounds eye of round steak, partially frozen, and sliced paper-thin against the grain

3 limes, quartered

1 bunch fresh Thai basil or cilantro (leaves only)

Fried Shallots (page 39) for garnish

Hoisin sauce (see page 22) for serving

Chili-garlic sauce (see page 21) for serving

Bring a large pot of water to a boil over high heat and cook the noodles until tender yet firm, about 10 seconds. Drain and divide among large soup bowls.

Meanwhile, in another large pot, bring the stock to a gentle boil over medium heat. About 5 minutes before serving, add the onion, and adjust the seasoning with fish sauce or salt, if necessary. Right before serving, raise the heat to high and bring the broth to a full boil.

Add some mung bean sprouts and layer a few beef slices over each serving of noodles. Ladle the piping hot broth along with some onion slices over the beef, making sure to cover the noodles. Taking a lime wedge or two, squeeze fresh lime juice into each bowl, and garnish with freshly torn basil or cilantro and fried shallots. Serve immediately with hoisin sauce and chili-garlic sauce on the side for dipping the beef.

## Variations

Substitute thinly sliced chicken for the beef. Cook the chicken after the noodles in the same cooking water. Top each serving of noodles with this poached chicken.

Substitute shrimp or squid cut into rings for the beef. Cook after the noodles in the same cooking water and serve over the noodles.

# RICE VERMICELLI WITH PORK AND SPRING ROLLS

Serves 6

In Cambodia, Laos, and Vietnam, rice noodles are often tossed with freshly torn or shredded lettuce leaves, shredded carrots, and sliced cucumber and then drizzled with scallion oil and a sweet and spicy fish sauce. The noodles are often topped with any number of grilled seafoods, such as shrimp and squid, or meats, such as pork or beef. Spring rolls are often added to the dish, cut up with scissors into small chunks. This is a refreshing noodle dish that will update your summer barbecue menu. I have no doubt the combination will become a favorite in no time.

¼ cup Basic Asian Marinade (page 43)

1 to 1½ pounds pork tenderloin, thinly sliced

Vegetable oil for brushing meat

1 pound fresh *bun*, or 8 ounces dried rice vermicelli soaked in water until pliable

2 romaine lettuce hearts, shredded

2 medium to large carrots, peeled and finely julienned or shredded

1 English or hothouse cucumber, peeled (optional), halved lengthwise, and thinly sliced crosswise

Fried Scallions in Oil (page 40)

1 bunch fresh mint (leaves only)

1 cup chopped unsalted dry-roasted peanuts

Fried Crab and Pork Spring Rolls (optional, page 157)

Sweet, Sour, and Spicy Fish Sauce (page 41)

18 long bamboo skewers, soaked in water for 20 minutes

Pour the marinade into a small to medium bowl, add the pork, and mix together well. Thread an equal amount on each skewer and marinate for 20 minutes. Brush each meat skewer with oil. Heat a well-oiled grill pan over medium-high heat and grill the skewered meat until crisped on both sides, about 5 minutes total.

Bring a large pot of water to a boil over high heat and cook the noodles until tender yet firm, about 5 to 10 seconds for either *bun* or dried vermicelli. Drain, shock under cold running water, and drain again. Transfer to a large mixing bowl, and add the lettuce, carrots, and cucumber. Toss and divide among large pasta plates or soup bowls. Garnish each serving with a generous amount of Fried Scallions in Oil.

Top each serving of noodles with 3 meat skewers. Instruct your guests to garnish their servings with some freshly torn mint leaves, crushed peanuts, and spring rolls, if using, and to drizzle Sweet, Sour, and Spicy Fish Sauce over the whole dish.

# STIR-FRIED BROAD RICE NOODLES WITH BEEF, BEAN SPROUTS, AND SCALLIONS

**Serves 6**

Fresh broad rice noodles are worth seeking out. Thick, rich, and slightly chewy, they can be stir-fried with beef, bean sprouts, and scallions, and seasoned with soy sauce for a simple, classic Chinese recipe.

The noodles are available in Chinese and Vietnamese markets. When stir-frying these noodles be sure to work in small batches—the noodles are less likely to stick together this way. Freeze the beef for 30 to 45 minutes for easy slicing. The amount of oil you use for stir-frying the noodles will depend on your cooking equipment. A cured wok or nonstick skillet will require less oil than a new wok or stainless steel skillet.

½ cup thin soy sauce

1 teaspoon tapioca or arrowroot starch

1 tablespoon dark sesame oil

1 ounce ginger, grated

1 large garlic clove, grated

1 pound beef sirloin or tenderloin, thinly sliced against the grain

⅓ to ½ cup vegetable oil

3 scallions, trimmed, halved lengthwise, and cut into 1-inch-long pieces

1 pound fresh broad rice noodles, cut into 1-inch-wide strips

1½ cups mung bean sprouts

Chili-garlic sauce (see page 21) for serving

In a medium bowl, stir together 2 tablespoons of the soy sauce and tapioca starch until smooth. Stir in the sesame oil, ginger, and garlic. Add the beef and mix well to coat evenly. Marinate for 20 minutes.

Heat 1 tablespoon of oil in a wok over high heat, and stir-fry a third of the scallions until fragrant, about 1 minute. Add a third of the beef and stir-fry until pink, about 2 minutes. Transfer to a plate. Add 1 to 2 tablespoons of oil to the same wok and stir-fry a third of the noodles, seasoning them with 2 tablespoons of the soy sauce. Stir-fry until the noodles are heated through, about 5 minutes. Return the beef and scallions to the wok and add ½ cup of the mung bean sprouts. Toss to mix well and cook for 1 to 2 minutes more. Toss, cook for 1 minute, and serve hot. Repeat the process 2 more times, splitting each batch into 2 servings. Serve with chili-garlic sauce to taste, on the side.

# STIR-FRIED RICE STICKS WITH TAMARIND SAUCE, DRIED SHRIMP, TOFU, SPROUTS, AND EGGS

**Serves 6**

Rice noodles can stick together, so a generous amount of oil generally eases the cooking. In this version of pad Thai, the rice noodles are stir-fried and seasoned with a sweet and tangy palm sugar and tamarind—based sauce. The salty elements of dried shrimp and fish sauce enhance the seasoning further. A squeeze or two of lime over the dish balances out the flavors.

Dried shrimp are labeled and sold by size: extra small, small, medium, and large. The small size noted here helps the shrimp blend nicely into the noodle mix. If you can only find large ones, just chop them. And if you can't find dried shrimp at all, add cooked shrimp or shredded leftover chicken for a fun take on the original. Pressed extra-firm tofu is sold, vacuum-sealed, in Asian markets and health food stores. Rubbery in texture, the cakes are about ½ inch thick and rectangular in shape. When sliced, they will not fall apart in the stir-fry, unlike other tofu cakes sold packed in water.

½ cup fish sauce

½ cup tamarind (liquid concentrate)

½ cup palm sugar or sugar

1 cup vegetable oil

1 large garlic clove, crushed, peeled, and minced

⅓ cup extra-small to small dried shrimp (about ½-inch-long tails); or 36 small headless tiger shrimp, peeled and deveined

2 pressed extra-firm tofu cakes, thinly sliced crosswise

6 large eggs

3 cups Basic Asian Stock (chicken, page 46)

8 to 10 ounces narrow or medium dried rice sticks, soaked in water until pliable

3 scallions, trimmed and thinly sliced on the diagonal

2½ cups mung bean sprouts

¾ cup chopped unsalted dry-roasted peanuts

2 limes, each sliced into 6 wedges

In a bowl, whisk together the fish sauce, tamarind, and sugar until the sugar is completely dissolved. Set the sauce aside.

Heat 2 tablespoons of the oil in a large skillet over high heat. Stir-fry the garlic until fragrant and just golden, about 1 minute. Add the dried shrimp, if using, and tofu and stir-fry until the tofu is lightly crisped, about 2 minutes. Transfer to a plate and set aside.

In the same skillet, heat 2 more tablespoons of the oil over high heat. Add the eggs, breaking the yokes by stirring lightly a couple of times. (Both white and yellow parts should be visible). Cook into an omelet (it should not be runny). Transfer to a plate, let cool, julienne, and set aside.

At this time, divide all of the ingredients into 6 equal portions.

If using fresh shrimp, bring a small to medium pot of water to a boil over high heat and blanch the tiger shrimp until opaque, about 1 minute. Shock them under cold running water and drain. Set the poached shrimp aside.

In the large skillet, cook each portion as follows: heat 2 tablespoons of oil over high heat. Add the chicken stock, sauce, and rice noodles. Cook until the noodles absorb the liquid fully. Add the tofu mixture and toss to distribute evenly. Transfer the noodles to a plate and garnish with omelet, scallions, bean sprouts, peanuts, and 2 lime wedges. Repeat the process 5 more times. Garnish with poached shrimp, if using.

# SILVER PIN NOODLES WITH CHICKEN, BEAN SPROUTS, AND SCALLIONS

**Serves 6**

Paris brings back memories of family gatherings for me, of expatriate Asian cooking, and of these special silver pin noodles. Upon special request, my Vietnamese uncle was always happy to prepare more than enough individual batches for our rather large family, stir-frying the tapered, 2-inch-long, hand-rolled noodles one serving at a time. He ran a veritable assembly line, cooking so quickly that nobody ever complained about the wait.

Like all stir-fry recipes, the idea here is never to overcrowd the wok, allowing the heat to travel freely around each ingredient. To serve 6, stir-fry 3 batches. Silver pin noodles are sold fresh (they are actually precooked) in the refrigerated section of Chinese and Vietnamese markets. In a pinch, for a slightly different texture, you can cut up fresh broad rice noodles, or use large dried rice sticks (soak these until pliable before stir-frying). Japanese udon, which is similar in texture to silver pins, makes an excellent substitute. Cut the noodles into 2- to 3-inch pieces.

6 tablespoons vegetable oil

3 scallions, trimmed, quartered lengthwise, and cut into 1-inch-long pieces

6 boneless skinless chicken thighs

1 pound fresh silver pin noodles

1½ cups mung bean sprouts

6 tablespoons thin soy sauce

Freshly ground black pepper

Heat 2 tablespoons of oil in a wok over high heat, and stir-fry a third of the scallions until wilted, about 1 minute. Add a third of the chicken and continue to stir-fry until cooked through, about 2 minutes. Add a third of the noodles and continue to stir-fry until the noodles are heated through and softened, about 5 minutes. Add ½ cup of the mung bean sprouts, 2 tablespoons of the soy sauce, and season with pepper to taste. Toss, cook for 1 minute, divide into 2 servings, and serve hot. Repeat twice more, splitting each batch into 2 servings.

# CELLOPHANE NOODLES

CHAPTER **8**

Made from mung bean starch or sweet potato starch, cellophane noodles are opaque when raw, and transparent when cooked. Their shiny transparency explains why they are called cellophane or glass noodles. My daughter smiles when she eats these, and calls them "magic noodles" because they change opacity in just a few minutes when cooking.

Cellophane noodles are versatile. Although flavorless on their own, they absorb flavor from any number of ingredients. Asians consider these noodles more like vegetables because they are derived from vegetables rather than grain. Perhaps that is why they are often served with a side of steamed rice, which is meant to complete the meal.

One of my fondest food memories of cellophane noodles is from time spent in Seoul, South Korea, where my interpreter and I shared meals while I was doing research for a project. I recall sitting down for a snack at the airport before I boarded the plane and flew back to New York. I wanted *chap chae*, a Korean stir-fried dish made with thick sweet potato noodles, beef, cabbage, and carrots. My newfound friend ordered the same, but she also asked for a bowl of rice on the side and said "*chap chae* is not good by itself." While I begged to differ, I understood that she meant the dish itself was not a complete meal.

When I eat a similar dish of Chinese origin—braised thin mung bean noodles with chicken, shrimp, shiitakes, and cabbage—I like the accompanying bowl of rice on the side. This is because mung bean noodles are much thinner than their Korean sweet potato cousins, and the dish just doesn't feel as hearty.

Chinese mung bean noodles are often employed for their chewy texture in stir-fries and clay pot dishes, and as filler for dumplings or spring rolls. They also appear in two very classic Southeast Asian specialties: The first is crab shells stuffed with a combination of cellophane noodles, ground pork, and crab. They are baked with butter, a European ingredient left over from the French colonial era. The second dish is a steamed pork pâté, which incorporates egg and anchovies into ground pork. (This, too, is French influenced, but tastes nothing like French pâté). Here noodle's main role is to add texture and otherwise fill the dish.

# CELLOPHANE NOODLE TYPES

**DANGMYEON:** This Korean cellophane noodle is made from sweet potato starch. Thicker and more chewy than the Chinese version (see above), the noodles are stir-fried and or braised. The Japanese use a similar noodle made of sweet potato starch as well.

**FEN SI:** This Chinese cellophane is very thin. Made of mung bean starch, it is bundled together with thin kitchen string and sold in small or large packs. This noodle is used in China and many parts of Southeast Asia. The word *si* in *fen si* means "thread." Indeed they are as thin as thread and are often labeled "mung bean threads" on the packaging as a result.

You will note that this chapter is shorter than the others in this book, but in the next chapter, cellophane noodles appear in Vegetable Dumplings (page 153) and Vietnamese spring rolls (page 157).

## SOME TIPS AND GUIDELINES

Cellophane noodles are always dried. They come thin or thick, and in small or large packages. They must be soaked in water until pliable before boiling, braising, stir-frying, or serving them in broth. When serving them in broth, be sure to boil them first. Never use hot water to soften the noodle: it softens them too much, preventing them from cooking evenly when stir-fried or served in soups.

Cellophane noodles are available in health food stores, the international food aisles of your supermarket, and any Asian market. The noodles made from sweet potato starch need to cook about 1 to 2 minutes longer than those made from mung bean starch.

# STEAMED MUNG BEAN NOODLES AND EGG PÂTÉ WITH GROUND PORK

**Serves 6**

This steamed cake made with mung bean cellophane noodles, ground pork, cloud ear mushrooms, and salted duck eggs is a childhood favorite. Each bite-size piece of pâté can be wrapped in lettuce, drizzled with Fried Scallions in Oil, and dipped in Sweet, Sour, and Spicy Fish Sauce. Or the pâté can be sliced and served over rice, drizzled with the sauce and scallions in oil. I like to serve it with an herbal soy sauce dip on the side as well.

Cloud ear mushrooms can be found in health food stores and in Asian markets. Salted duck eggs are also sold in Asian markets. They are packaged in three different ways: in clear plastic jars filled with brine, in white foam boxes labeled with a picture of eggs with deep orange yolks, or in large clay pots. The eggs in the clay pots are covered and preserved in salted black ash. To make your own salted eggs, see the Note below and begin a month before making this dish. You can also use fresh chicken eggs and add anchovies to the mix. The salty element is what makes the dish.

6 salted duck eggs or salted chicken eggs (see Note), beaten

2 anchovy fillets, bones removed, and fillets mashed

2.5 ounces mung bean noodles, soaked in water until pliable and coarsely chopped

8 ounces coarsely ground pork

6 small to medium cloud ears, soaked in water until pliable and minced

2 large heads Boston lettuce, leaves separated

Fried Scallions in Oil (page 40) for serving

Sweet, Sour, and Spicy Fish Sauce (page 41) for serving

In a mixing bowl, mix together the eggs, anchovies, cellophane noodles, ground pork, and cloud ears until well combined. Divide the mixture into 6 oiled, small, heat-proof bowls or individual soufflé dishes, and set them on a rack of a large bamboo steamer. (You may have to steam them in two batches.) Fill a wok halfway with water and place the bamboo steamer on top. Cover, bring to a boil over high heat, and steam the pâtés until set and cooked through, 15 to 20 minutes.

To eat, spoon some pâté onto a lettuce leaf. Drizzle with some Fried Scallions in Oil, roll up, and dip in the Sweet, Sour, and Spicy Fish Sauce.

**NOTE:** To make your own salted eggs, boil 3 cups of water with ½ cup of salt. Let the brine cool completely (refrigerate to speed the process, if you wish). Carefully fit as many raw chicken eggs into a 1-quart glass jar as you can, and pour the brine over them. Refrigerate for 1 month, or until the eggs are well salted. The longer they sit, the more salty they will be.

# MUNG BEAN NOODLE, PORK, CILANTRO, AND CUCUMBER SOUP

**Serves 6**

This is a simple ground pork noodle soup. When I was a child, my mother would make a soup with pork, cucumber, and cilantro for us. It was a delicious, quick meal made with readily available items. It was comfort food for my brothers and me when we were sick. In the 1970s, there was not much in the way of Asian ingredients available in the United States, but cilantro, ginger, and soy sauce could be found. Years later, I stumbled upon a Thai recipe that included not only ground pork and cilantro, but cellophane noodles as well. This is my interpretation of that classic soup. Fried garlic adds a delicious sweet note to the finish.

2½ quarts Basic Asian Stock (pork or chicken, page 46)

1 to 1½ pounds coarsely ground pork

1    bunch fresh cilantro, stemmed and coarsely chopped

1    English cucumber, peeled, halved lengthwise, cored, and sliced ¼ inch thick

3.75 ounces mung bean noodles, soaked in water until pliable and drained

Fried Garlic in Oil (page 39) for serving

In a medium to large pot, bring the stock to a boil over high heat. Put about ¼ cup of pork in a ladle. Lower it into the soup stock, breaking up the meat with the back of a spoon and releasing it into the stock. Repeat until all of the meat is added to the stock. Add the cilantro and cucumber, cover, lower the heat to medium-low, and keep warm until ready to serve.

Bring a pot of water to a boil and cook the cellophane noodles in the water until completely transparent, about 1 minute. Drain and divide among large soup bowls. Add stock with ground meat and cilantro to each serving of noodles. Garnish with the garlic oil, including bits of fried garlic.

# STIR-FRIED SWEET POTATO NOODLES WITH VEGETABLES AND BEEF

**Serves 6**

*Chap chae* is a classic Korean dish made with sweet potato cellophane noodles. These are two to three times as thick as their Chinese counterpart, which is made with mung bean starch. Stir-fried with vegetables and julienned beef, it is a perfect light meal. A small amount of julienned beef is traditionally added to the dish, but ground beef is a delicious alternative, allowing the cook to distribute the flavorful meat throughout the dish. Try it either way.

Eight ounces of meat is plenty, but add more for a heartier meal. For interesting variations, substitute chicken or pork for the beef. Chinese mung bean noodles can be used here, but note that they will cook in half as much time. Freeze the beef for 30 to 45 minutes for easy slicing.

Bring a medium pot of water to a boil over high heat, and cook the noodles until tender but still chewy, 2 to 3 minutes. Drain, shock under cold running water, and drain again. Set aside.

In a bowl combine the soy sauce, sesame oil, and sugar, and whisk until the sugar dissolves completely. Take 2 tablespoons of the sauce and use to marinate the beef in a separate bowl.

Heat 1 tablespoon of the oil in a large skillet over high heat. Stir-fry the garlic and carrots for 10 seconds. Add the shiitakes and spinach and stir-fry until just wilted, about 1 minute. Transfer the vegetable stir-fry to a plate. Add another tablespoon of oil to the skillet and stir-fry the marinated meat, breaking it up (especially if using ground beef) until just cooked, about 1 minute. Add to the vegetable stir-fry. Add the remaining tablespoon of oil to the skillet and stir-fry the noodles with the remaining sauce, tossing to coat evenly. Reduce the heat to medium, return the vegetables and meat to the skillet, season with pepper to taste, and toss to combine well. Transfer to a serving platter, and garnish with scallions and sesame seeds.

---

12 ounces dried sweet potato noodles, soaked in water until pliable

⅓ cup thin soy sauce

1 tablespoon dark sesame oil

2 tablespoons sugar

8 to 12 ounces beef sirloin, thinly sliced and julienned, or coarsely ground

3 tablespoons vegetable oil

1 large garlic clove, minced

1 medium carrot, peeled and cut into 2-inch-long matchsticks

10 shiitake mushrooms, stemmed, and caps julienned

1 pound baby spinach

Freshly ground black pepper

1 scallion, trimmed and thinly sliced on the diagonal

Toasted sesame seeds for garnish

# STUFFED CRAB SHELLS

**Serves 12**

Called *cua farci* in Vietnamese, these stuffed crab shells make for an excellent appetizer or a light meal when served with a salad on the side. The dish reflects a French influence: The word *farci* is French for "stuffed," for example, and the dish contains butter. But it is very much Vietnamese in flavor and texture. After you have enjoyed Atlantic blue crabs or small stone crabs (with black claws) in other dishes, scrub the shells and save them to make this dish. Otherwise, you can use individual soufflé dishes or ramekins.

1.25 ounces mung bean noodles (1 small bundle), soaked in water until pliable

4 large fresh shiitake mushrooms, stemmed and caps minced

12 ounces coarsely ground pork

1 pound lump crabmeat

1 large shallot, minced

1 large garlic clove, minced

2 large eggs, lightly beaten

Kosher salt and freshly ground black pepper

12 Atlantic blue crab shells, about 5 inches from point to point

½ cup (1 stick) butter, cut into 24 thin slices

Fried Scallions in Oil (page 40) for serving

Sweet, Sour, and Spicy Fish Sauce (page 41) for serving

Preheat the oven to 375°F.

Drain the noodles, then chop them and put them in a large bowl. Add the shiitakes, pork, crabmeat, shallot, garlic, and eggs. Add salt and pepper to taste. Toss to combine the ingredients thoroughly.

Divide the stuffing equally among the 12 crab shells (or ramekins), smoothing out the top. Place 2 pats of butter (next to one another) on top of each serving, and bake until golden, 15 to 20 minutes.

Spoon some scallion oil (including scallions) on top of each stuffed crab. Serve with Sweet, Sour, and Spicy Fish Sauce on the side, and instruct guests to drizzle some sauce over the stuffed crabs.

# SPICY SWEET POTATO NOODLES AND KIMCHI STEW

**Serves 6**

6 cups *Kombu Dashi* (kelp stock, page 51)

⅓ cup thin soy sauce

⅓ cup sake

3 scallions, trimmed and cut into 1½ -inch pieces

2 ounces ginger, thinly sliced

3 cups chopped kimchi

12 dried medium shiitake mushrooms, soaked in water until pliable, stemmed, and quartered

12 ounces sweet potato noodles, soaked in water until pliable and drained

I love kimchi. This spicy pickled cabbage, a specialty of South Korea, is eaten with just about every meal in that country. Koreans often joke that they never leave home without it, and this is basically true. While flying from Korea to the United States one time, I noticed a garlicky smell in the plane. Several Korean passengers had brought along homemade kimchi just in case the meal service didn't include it. Definitely proud with garlic, this table condiment is sometimes added to stews like this one, which includes chewy and slippery potato starch noodles. Note: Kimchi is sold in Korean or Japanese markets, and in some health food stores. In a pinch, chopped Napa cabbage and 1 to 2 tablespoons of chili-garlic sauce make a quick-and-tasty substitute.

In a medium pot, combine the kelp stock, soy sauce, sake, scallions, ginger, kimchi, and mushrooms. Bring to a boil over high heat. Add the noodles and cook for an additional 3 minutes. Serve immediately.

# BRAISED MUNG BEAN NOODLES WITH CABBAGE AND SHIITAKES

**Serves 6**

Here, cellophane noodles made from mung bean starch are braised in chicken stock seasoned with soy sauce and sesame oil, and they absorb all of those good flavors. Enhanced further by such pungent, earthy ingredients as dried shiitake mushrooms, fresh ginger, scallions, and dried shrimp, this noodle dish is sure to become a favorite. The dried shrimp can be found in Asian markets, or omitted altogether.

2 tablespoons vegetable oil

1 large garlic clove, minced

1 ounce ginger, grated

2 scallions, trimmed and cut into 1½-inch pieces

6 medium to large dried shiitake mushrooms, soaked in water until pliable, stemmed, and caps julienned

¼ cup small dried shrimp (optional)

About 6 large Napa cabbage leaves, cut into 1-inch pieces

2.5 ounces dried mung bean noodles, soaked in water until pliable and drained

1½ cups Chinese Superior Stock (page 47)

1 tablespoon or more thin soy sauce

1 teaspoon dark sesame oil

Freshly ground black pepper

Heat the oil in a medium pot over medium-high heat. Stir-fry the garlic, ginger, and scallions until fragrant, about 1 minute. Add the shiitakes, dried shrimp (if using) and the cabbage and continue to stir-fry until wilted and golden, about 5 minutes. Add the noodles and toss to distribute the ingredients evenly. Add the stock, soy sauce, sesame oil, and black pepper to taste. Reduce the heat to low, cover the pot, and braise for 6 to 8 minutes, until the noodles have completely absorbed the liquid.

# BUNS, DUMPLINGS, AND SPRING ROLLS

  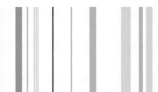

It may seem curious to include buns, dumplings (including wontons), and spring rolls in this book, but in Asian food cultures, they belong in the noodle category. Flour, water, and salt are the basic ingredients here, just as they are in noodles. And like noodles, they are considered snacks and simple one-dish meals. Buns can be steamed or baked and eaten for breakfast or a quick lunch. Dumplings can be steamed or boiled, pan-fried or deep-fried, or served in broth; they are enjoyed at lunch or dinner. The same goes for the beautiful, lacy, crispy crêpes and spring rolls. And all of these can be served as an appetizer or full meal, filled with meat, seafood, vegetables, or combinations of these. One of the best confidence-building tips you will pick up here is that all the dumpling fillings are interchangeable.

It is hard to pinpoint exactly when these delicate foods first appeared. Regional preferences, however, are easy to discern. The Cantonese, in southern China, pride themselves on making the thinnest wrappers possible and the most delicate dumplings. These are generally referred to as *dim sum*, which translates as "touch of the heart." Northern-style dumplings have thick wrappers, and while delicious, they are heavier than southern dumplings. It is generally believed that the great variety of dumplings in the south grew out of tea houses, where men socialized. Tea is still drunk in great quantities in China. To this day it is not unusual to see simple little huts along a country road where you can pull over and have tea, a smoke, and a chat. Food was eventually introduced to this ritual, and most of the huts became more elaborate.

What started as a few offerings grew into literally hundreds of types of dumplings, which filled food carts, menus, and all the associated trappings. Tea houses eventually became the dim sum restaurants of today. Dim sum is so rooted in the ritual of tea drinking that when people say "*yam cha*" ("drink tea") they really mean "Let's go have dim sum." My family and I often have dim sum on Sunday mornings, when you can take the time to relax and enjoy the slow pace of the meal.

In this chapter I include all sorts of wonderful recipes. There are dumplings with plain wheat wrappers and others with egg wrappers, including wontons (page 147). There are wonderful fillings, like pork and watercress (page 150). In addition to dumplings, there are recipes for Vietnamese spring rolls (page 157) as well as summer rolls (fresh, uncooked spring rolls, page 158). And there is a recipe for classic Chinese egg rolls that can also be used to make spring rolls (page 159). A filling of cabbage, carrots, and shiitakes is wrapped in a thick, egg-based wrapper for egg rolls and in a thin, almost translucent wheat wrapper for spring rolls.

# FREEZING AND COOKING DUMPLINGS

Dumplings and spring rolls are fun to make. Most can be stored in the freezer for up to 3 months. The notable exception is anything with a tofu stuffing, which should be eaten the day it's made. When frozen, tofu separates.

Freeze freshly assembled dumplings (including wontons) in a single layer on a cookie sheet, preventing one from touching the other, or about 1/8 inch apart. Once the dumplings are frozen solid, transfer them to a resealable plastic bag and return to the freezer immediately until ready to cook. There is no need to thaw before cooking. A terrific thing about these foods is that whether you grab six or six dozen from the freezer, they can go from freezer to stove to table in minutes. Just add a dipping sauce. My four-year-old daughter goes to the freezer, opens a bag, grabs a couple of handfuls, and then says, "I want this for dinner."

Freshly made dumplings can be steamed, boiled, deep-fried, or pan-fried. To steam dumplings, all you need is an inexpensive bamboo steaming rack and lid set in or atop a wok filled halfway up with water. Line the steaming rack with a single layer of lettuce or Napa cabbage leaves (to keep it clean between batches). Set the dumplings on top in a single layer, being sure to keep them from touching. Cover, bring the water to a boil over high heat, and steam the dumplings until done, usually about 5 minutes.

Dumplings can be boiled in a conventional saucepan or other suitably large pan. Boil the water first, and then add the dumplings. They are almost done when they float; give them 1 or 2 minutes more if they contain heavy fillings like meat.

Deep-fried dumplings are prepared by carefully lowering the dumplings into oil that is heated to 360°F to 375°F. They take about 3 to 5 minute to cook, and they crisp up nicely.

Pan-fried dumplings are called pot stickers, which, as the name indicates, tend to stick to the bottom of the pan. These are immensely popular wherever they are served, and they appear on both authentic Chinese and adjusted Chinese-American restaurant menus. The secret is simple: use a skillet with a lid so that you can steam and pan-fry the dumpling simultaneously. Choose a large nonstick skillet and add equal parts water and oil (about 2 tablespoons of each) for the first batch, heating them over medium-high. When the oil starts to sizzle and the water bubbles, add the dumplings, plump side down. Cook, covered, for about 5 minutes. The water will evaporate, leaving behind the hot oil, which will brown and crisp the dumplings and cause them to stick to the pan slightly. You will need to add the same amount of water to cook each batch of pot stickers, but you will only need to add oil to the pan with every other batch. Crispy on the outside and tender and juicy on the inside, these will become family favorites.

Steamed or boiled dumplings such as wontons can be served floating in a fragrant broth like Chinese Superior Stock (page 47).

Whether you boil or deep-fry, always cook frozen dumplings in small batches—no more than 12 at a time—so as not to cool down the boiling water or hot oil too quickly.

# ASIAN WRAPPERS

Fresh wonton, dumpling, and egg roll wrappers can be found in health food stores in the refrigerated section. They should be kept refrigerated and consumed within 2 days of purchase. Dried rice papers can be found in the international aisle of your supermarket as well as in health food stores. Dried noodles should be kept in a dark cool place and consumed within 6 months.

**BANH TRANG:** These Vietnamese rice papers are brittle and translucent. Although usually round, they are sometimes triangular in shape. They should be soaked in water until pliable before forming spring rolls, which can be deep-fried or served fresh. These are a specialty ingredient in the cooking of Southeast Asia, including Vietnam, Cambodia, and Laos.

**DUMPLING WRAPPERS:** Round or square, dumpling wrappers are used to make all sorts of bite-size foods that can be steamed, deep-fried, or pan-fried. Dumpling wrappers are made with or without egg or yellow food coloring and can range in color from whitish-beige (natural) to yellow. Use wheat wrappers for northern-style Chinese dumplings and egg wrappers for the thinner southern-style ones. These wrappers can also be cut into strips and stir-fried.

**EGG ROLL WRAPPERS:** These are used for making the traditional Cantonese egg rolls. You can also cut these into strips the width of fettuccini and stir-fry them as you would egg noodles.

Finally, I also provide recipes for hearty buns filled with meat, which can be steamed or baked. The wonderful sweet pork bun called *char siu bao* is perhaps the best-known baked bun in Asian cooking. Filled with leftover barbecued or roast pork, these tasty little clouds of flavor are great on-the-go appetizers or snacks.

The recipes in this chapter make for wonderful social occasions when you want to try something different. Fried dumplings and spring rolls are especially well suited for cocktail parties and are delicious served with a soy sauce– or fish sauce–based dipping sauce, and chili-garlic sauce on the side for dipping.

Dumplings and rolls are fun to make with friends and family in large batches assembly-line style because everyone gets to participate at his or her own best level and then take some home.

I've stayed away from flatbreads that are derived from noodle dough because they seem a bit far afield, but I have given you a recipe for crêpes, which, like buns, dumplings, and spring rolls, are filled. Besides, crêpes are simple and great fun, and these are special: they are made with rice flour instead of all-purpose, and coconut milk rather than cow's milk.

The following are some of my favorite dumpling, spring roll, and bun recipes. The fillings are interchangeable; when you feel comfortable enough with the technique for assembling these, feel free to experiment with your favorite meat, seafood, or vegetable filling.

# PORK AND SHRIMP WONTONS

**Serves 6; makes 72 wontons**

One of my greatest joys when I was a young teenager was to go to New York's Chinatown with my dad. I often craved wontons, but not from just any old place. It had to be that tiny little hole–in–the–wall restaurant on Mott Street. Expert at marketing, the wily owner placed the cook and his huge deep wok in the front window. After a few moments of watching this guy work, boiling and scooping out the noodles and wontons to order, you were sold. You just had to go in and have a bowl. The restaurant is still there today, and so is its signature dish: a sesame oil–infused chicken broth with a cluster of wildly delicious sweet pork and shrimp wontons floating on top. A little chili oil on the side, some steamed Chinese broccoli or *choy sum*, and I was in heaven. I'm still in heaven when I eat there all these many years later. For a tasty way to use these, try Egg Noodles with Wonton Soup and Asian Greens (page 77).

2 teaspoons dark sesame oil

2 tablespoons thin soy sauce, plus extra for serving

1 tablespoon tapioca starch or cornstarch

Kosher salt and freshly ground black pepper

1½ pounds small headless tiger shrimp, peeled, deveined, and minced

8 ounces coarsely ground pork

72 square or round wonton wrappers

Chili-garlic sauce (see page 21) for serving (optional)

In a bowl, stir together the sesame oil, soy sauce, and tapioca starch until well blended. Adjust the seasoning with salt and pepper. Add the shrimp and pork and mix thoroughly.

Take a wrapper and put a heaping teaspoon of pork mixture in the center. Dab the edge lightly with water and seal to form a half-moon (if using a round wrapper) or triangle (if using a square). Bring the two ends together, dabbing each with water, and pressing one end over the other, so the wonton resembles a hat. Continue in this way until all of the wontons have been filled and sealed. Place on a cookie sheet lined with wax paper (not parchment paper), making sure they do not touch.

Bring a large pot of water to a boil over high heat. In batches, cook the wontons until they float to the top and are cooked through, about 3 minutes. Using a slotted spoon, remove the wontons from the pot and divide among large soup bowls or plates. To eat, dip them in soy sauce, with chili-garlic sauce stirred in, if you wish.

# SWEET PORK BUNS

**Makes 12 large or
24 small buns**

These sweet pork buns, or *bao*, are traditionally made with leftover Cantonese roast pork, but you can use leftover Western–style pork. You also have an option of baking the buns instead of steaming them. The dough requires yeast and will need to rise for at least 3 hours. Working with yeast dough can be tricky, but this one is made with baker's yeast, which is not as sensitive to temperature as dry granulated yeast. Baker's yeast is also called wet yeast, compressed yeast, and block yeast. It is sold in large chunks and in premeasured cubes wrapped in foil. It must be kept refrigerated until you are ready to use it. All packaged yeast, whether wet or dry, is dated. Though Shaoxing rice wine is used to flavor the pork filling, the more readily available Japanese rice wine called sake will do nicely.

2    teaspoons baker's yeast

2    cups lukewarm water

4    cups all-purpose flour, plus
     extra for kneading

3    tablespoons sugar

2    teaspoons baking powder

1    teaspoon kosher salt

3    tablespoons oil

1    pound finely diced leftover
     cooked pork

If you're making the larger steamed buns, cut out 12 pieces of parchment paper, each 2 inches square. For the smaller buns, cut 24 pieces, each 1½ inches square. (If you're going to bake the buns, you will use a sheet of parchment paper.)

Combine the yeast and water in a measuring cup and stir well.

In a large mixing bowl, sift together the flour, sugar, baking powder, and salt. Make a well and add the yeast water. With a spoon, stir from the center out, gradually working the flour mixture into the well until a dough forms. Turn out the dough onto a generously floured work surface and knead with floured hands until the dough is elastic and smooth, about 10 minutes. Shape the soft dough into a ball.

Grease a large mixing bowl with 2 tablespoons of the oil. Put the dough inside, rolling it a couple of times to grease the dough all around. Cover with a damp kitchen towel and allow to rise at room temperature or slightly warmer for 3 to 4 hours.

Meanwhile, in a wok over high heat, add the remaining tablespoon of oil and stir-fry the pork with scallions until heated through, about 2 minutes. Add the rice wine, oyster sauce, soy sauce, sugar, and sesame oil, and continue to stir-fry to mix the ingredients well. Remove from the heat and allow the filling to cool completely.

Cut the dough into 12 or 24 equal pieces. Roll each piece into a ball, and keep them apart from each other but covered with the same damp towel, to keep the dough from drying out as you work with one piece at a time.

Take a piece of dough and flatten it out into a thick disk, resembling a round wonton wrapper in shape, but about ⅛ inch thick. Place about 2 teaspoons

2   scallions, trimmed and finely
    chopped

¼   cup rice wine

2½  tablespoons oyster sauce

2½  tablespoons thin soy sauce

1   tablespoon sugar

1½  teaspoons dark sesame oil

1   large egg (if baking the buns)

of meat in the center of the dough for the small bun, and 2 tablespoons for larger buns.

To steam the buns: Bring up and pinch together two opposite edges of the dough. Then pinch the other two edges together. Place the bun seam side up on a piece of parchment paper. Repeat to make a total of 12 or 24 buns. Fill a wok halfway with water and bring to a boil over high heat. Fill each rack of a steamer with buns, setting them 2 inches apart, with the paper side down. Set the steamer on the wok and steam for 15 to 20 minutes, depending on the size of the bun. Test by inserting a skewer in the center and making sure it comes out hot and clear of raw dough.

To bake the buns: Preheat the oven to 375°F, and line a baking sheet with parchment paper. Gather the edges of the filled dough in the center, pinching them together to secure and enclose the filling completely. Place the buns seam side down on the baking sheet, about 2 inches apart. In a small bowl whisk the egg with 2 tablespoons water. Brush each bun lightly with the egg wash and bake for 15 to 20 minutes. Insert a skewer as instructed above to test for doneness.

**CHICKEN AND CABBAGE BUNS:** Once you know how to make the dough for Chinese buns, the possibilities for fillings are endless. Here is one that I like to make occasionally. While the dough is rising, heat 1 tablespoon of oil in a wok over high heat. Stir-fry 1 ounce of grated ginger and 2 chopped scallions until fragrant, about 1 minute. Add 1 pound of coarsely ground or finely chopped boneless skinless chicken thighs and continue to stir-fry until opaque, about 3 minutes. Add 8 medium to large cabbage leaves, minced; 8 fresh shiitake mushroom caps, minced; and ½ cup of Basic Asian Marinade (page 43), and cook until the juices have evaporated and the cabbage is lightly browned, 10 to 15 minutes. Remove from the heat and allow the filling to cool completely. Then proceed with the recipe.

# PORK AND WATERCRESS DUMPLINGS

Serves 6;
makes 72 dumplings

I love the combination of sweet pork and peppery watercress, especially when chopped and folded into a dumpling. Boiled, steamed, or pan-fried, these delicious morsels can be dipped in a combination of soy sauce and chili-garlic sauce. Like many dumplings, these freeze beautifully, so it pays to make a lot of them. (See page 145 for freezing instructions.)

2   teaspoons dark sesame oil

2   tablespoons thin soy sauce, plus extra for serving

1   tablespoon tapioca starch or cornstarch

Freshly ground black pepper

1¼ pounds coarsely ground pork

8   ounces watercress or pea shoots, trimmed and minced

72  round round wheat dumpling wrappers

Chili-garlic sauce (see page 21) for serving (optional)

In a large bowl, stir together the sesame oil, soy sauce, and tapioca starch until well blended. Season with pepper to taste. Add the pork and watercress and mix thoroughly.

Take a wrapper and put a heaping teaspoon of pork mixture in the center. Dab the edge lightly with water and seal to form a half-moon, pressing any air out. Place the dumplings, flat side down, on a cookie sheet lined with wax paper, making sure they do not touch.

Bring a large pot of water to a boil over high heat. Cook the dumplings in batches until they float to the top. Remove from the heat and wait 1 or 2 minutes to make sure the filling is cooked. Scoop out the dumplings with a slotted spoon and divide among large soup plates. Or steam, pan-fry, or deep-fry the dumplings (see page 145) if you prefer.

To eat, dip the dumplings in the soy sauce and chili garlic sauce, if desired.

# BEEF AND SCALLION DUMPLINGS

**Serves 6;**
**makes 72 dumplings**

Beef and scallion dumplings are deliciously rich and peppery. For a more authentic flavor, try these with Chinese garlic chives (with or without their flowering buds), which can be found in Asian markets. Garlic chives tend to be milder than either scallions or garlic.

In a medium bowl, stir together the sesame oil, soy sauce, and tapioca starch until well blended. Adjust the seasoning with salt and pepper to taste. Add the beef and scallions and mix thoroughly.

2   teaspoons dark sesame oil

2   tablespoons thin soy sauce, plus extra for serving

1   tablespoon tapioca starch or cornstarch

Kosher salt and freshly ground black pepper

2   pounds coarsely ground beef

4   scallions, trimmed and minced

72  round wheat dumpling wrappers

Chili-garlic sauce (see page 21) for serving (optional)

Take a wrapper and put a heaping teaspoon of beef mixture in the center. Dab the edge lightly with water and seal to form a half-moon. Place the dumplings, flat side down, on a cookie sheet lined with wax paper, making sure they do not touch.

Bring a large pot of water to a boil over high heat. Cook the dumplings in batches until they float to the top. Remove from the heat and wait 1 or 2 minutes to make sure the filling is cooked. Scoop out the dumplings with a slotted spoon and divide among large soup plates. Or steam, pan-fry, or deep-fry the dumplings (see page 145) if you prefer.

To eat, dip the dumplings in the soy sauce and chili garlic sauce mixture, if you wish.

# TOFU AND SHIITAKE MUSHROOM DUMPLINGS

**Serves 6;
makes 72 dumplings**

Tofu and shiitake mushroom dumplings are light. Their signature mildly smoky flavor comes from the dried shiitakes. Firm to extra-firm tofu is preferred for added texture. (Avoid pressed tofu, which is sold vacuum-sealed.) Unlike meat or seafood dumplings, the tofu ones do not freeze well at all. Cook and serve fresh. These are subtle in flavor with only a hint of dark sesame oil.

2   teaspoons dark sesame oil

2   tablespoons thin soy sauce,
    plus extra for serving

2   pounds firm to extra-firm tofu,
    crushed

10  medium to large shiitake mush-
    rooms, stemmed and minced

Freshly ground black pepper

72  round wonton wrappers

In a bowl, stir together the sesame oil and soy sauce. Add the tofu and mushrooms and mix thoroughly. Season with pepper to taste.

Place a bowl of water on your work surface. Take a round wrapper and put about 2 teaspoons of the filling in the center. Dip your finger in the water and dab the edge of the wrapper lightly with water and seal to form a half-moon, pressing any air out. Set the dumplings, flat side down, on a cookie sheet lined with wax paper, making sure they do not touch.

Bring a large pot of water to a boil over high heat. Cook the dumplings in batches until they float to the top. Remove from the heat and wait 1 or 2 minutes to make sure the filling is cooked. Scoop out the dumplings with a slotted spoon and divide among large soup plates. Or steam, pan-fry, or deep-fry the dumplings (see page 145) if you prefer.

Serve with soy sauce on the side for dipping, if desired.

# VEGETABLE DUMPLINGS

Serves 6;
makes 72 dumplings

Steamed or boiled vegetable dumplings are some of my favorites. These light morsels often contain cellophane noodles, shiitake mushrooms, and any number of leafy green vegetables (for example, spinach, bok choy, or Chinese broccoli). Sometimes shredded carrot is added for color. Wrapped in a thin round wheat wrapper, they are shaped into half-moons. Steam or boil them, or pan-fry to make pot stickers. They are delicious dipped in a combination of soy sauce and chili–garlic sauce.

⅓ cup plus 1 tablespoon thin soy sauce, plus extra for serving

2 tablespoons vegetable oil

2 ounces ginger, finely julienned

2 scallions, trimmed and finely chopped

1 or 2 red Thai chilies, stemmed, seeded, and thinly sliced into rounds

1 bunch fresh cilantro (leaves only)

1.25 ounces mung bean noodles (1 small bundle), soaked in water until pliable, drained, and finely chopped

12 large dried shiitake mushrooms, soaked in water until pliable, stemmed, and caps minced

8 ounces leafy greens, such as spinach, bok choy, or pea shoots, minced

1 tablespoon dark sesame oil

Freshly ground black pepper

72 round wheat or egg wrappers

Put all but 1 tablespoon of the soy sauce in a heat-proof bowl.

In a skillet, heat the oil over medium heat and stir-fry the ginger, scallions, and chilies until fragrant and golden, about 2 minutes. Add the cilantro and stir-fry until wilted. Add the stir-fry to the soy sauce, including the fragrant oil, and stir and set aside.

In a medium bowl, toss the noodles, mushrooms, greens, the remaining ⅓ cup of soy sauce, the sesame oil, and the pepper to taste, until well combined.

Place a bowl of water on your work surface. Take a round wrapper and put a heaping teaspoon of the filling in the center. Dip your finger in the water and dab the edge of the wrapper lightly with water, and seal to form a half-moon, pressing any air out. Set the dumplings, flat side down, on a cookie sheet lined with wax paper, making sure they do not touch.

Bring a large pot of water to a boil over high heat. Cook the dumplings in batches until they float to the top. Remove from the heat and wait 1 or 2 minutes to make sure the filling is cooked. Scoop out the dumplings with a slotted spoon and divide among large soup plates. Or steam, pan-fry, or deep-fry the dumplings (see page 145) if you prefer.

Serve with soy sauce on the side for dipping, if desired.

# CRISPY RICE FLOUR CRÊPES WITH BEAN SPROUTS AND MUSHROOMS

Serves 6;
makes about 12 crêpes

*Banh xeo* is the onomatopoeic Vietnamese name for these crêpes, derived from the sizzling sound the batter makes as it hits the hot surface of the crêpe pan. Delicately lacy, they can be filled with all sorts of ingredients. Almost any filling works. The batter comprises coconut milk, rice flour, and a hint of yellow turmeric for color. As your pan gets hot, you may have to sacrifice the first couple of crêpes and offer them up to the kitchen gods. If you use a 10-inch crêpe pan and have beginner's luck, you may actually get 14 to 15 crêpes.

3  tablespoons plus more vegetable oil

10  medium to large fresh shiitake mushrooms, stemmed and caps julienned

2  cups mung bean sprouts

Kosher salt and freshly ground black pepper

1½ cups rice flour

1 or 2 pinches turmeric

½ cup unsweetened coconut milk

1  large head Boston lettuce, leaves separated

1  bunch mint (leaves only)

2  medium to large carrots, peeled and finely julienned

1  English cucumber, peeled (optional), halved lengthwise, and thinly sliced

Sweet, Sour, and Spicy Fish Sauce (page 41) for serving

Heat 1 tablespoon oil in a wok over high heat, and stir-fry the mushrooms until wilted, 1 to 2 minutes. Add the bean sprouts, lightly toss, and transfer to a plate to cool. Season lightly with salt and pepper to taste.

In a medium bowl, whisk together the flour, turmeric, coconut milk, and the remaining 2 tablespoons of oil until smooth.

Heat a crêpe pan over medium-high heat, brushing it with oil. Add ¼ cup batter, swirling the pan to distribute the batter across the surface of the pan evenly. Cook until set and crispy, 3 to 5 minutes. Once the edges start lifting up, the crêpe is just about ready. Scatter a handful of stir-fried mushrooms and mung beans on one half of the crêpe and fold over the other half, as you would when making an omelet. Slide onto a plate. Make only as many crêpes as there are guests, and make seconds upon request. These are best when freshly made.

Garnish each crêpe with freshly torn lettuce leaves and mint, carrots, and cucumber and serve with Sweet, Sour, and Spicy Fish Sauce on the side. Instruct guests to drizzle about 2 tablespoons of the sauce over their crêpe.

An alternative way to serve this crêpe is to break off a piece and wrap it in a whole lettuce leaf along with some mint, carrots, and cucumber. Held between your fingers, this lettuce roll can then be dipped in the sauce.

# FRIED CRAB AND PORK SPRING ROLLS

**Serves 6;
makes 48 spring rolls**

Vietnamese spring rolls are everyone's favorite in my family. Wrapped in rice paper, they are deep-fried until golden and crisp. A bite reveals a chewy and tender filling of cellophane noodles, ground pork (and sometimes crabmeat), carrot, shallot, and garlic. Dipped in *nuoc cham* sauce, the ubiquitous Vietnamese table condiment made with fish sauce, each spring roll is wrapped in a tender lettuce leaf with mint, carrot, and cucumber.

1.25 ounces mung bean noodles
(1 small bundle), soaked in
water until pliable, drained,
and finely chopped

10 ounces coarsely ground pork,
or 5 ounces pork plus 5 ounces
lump crabmeat

2 tablespoons dried cloud ears,
soaked in water until softened,
drained, and minced

2 small carrots, peeled and
shredded

1 large shallot, minced

1 large egg, beaten

Kosher salt and freshly ground
black pepper

12 large round rice papers (about
6 to 8 inches in diameter),
quartered

Vegetable oil for deep-frying

2 heads Boston lettuce, leaves
separated, ribs trimmed

1 small cucumber, peeled, halved
lengthwise, seeded, and thinly
sliced into half-moons

1 bunch fresh mint (leaves only)

Sweet, Sour, and Spicy Fish Sauce
(page 41) for serving

Prepare Sweet, Sour, and Spicy Fish Sauce (see page 41) using half of the garlic called for in the recipe. Let the dipping sauce stand and allow the flavors to deepen.

In a large mixing bowl, mix together the noodles, pork, crabmeat, if using, cloud ears, half the carrots, the remaining garlic, the shallot, and egg until well combined. Season with salt and pepper.

Fill a rectangular baking pan halfway with lukewarm water. Arrange a lint-free kitchen towel on your work surface. Have a second lint-free kitchen towel for blotting. Soak 2 to 3 rice paper triangles in the water, one at a time, until pliable. Place the rice paper on the towel, which will absorb the excess water from the underside, while you blot the top with the second towel. (The idea is to work with a sticky, rather than slippery, rice paper.) On each rice paper, place a heaping tablespoon of the filling so it's off center and a bit closer to you. Shape the filling into a small sausage. Rolling tightly and carefully so as not to break the paper, fold the point of the paper closest to you over the filling. Fold in the sides and continue to roll to the end. Place each roll on a plate in a single layer, seam side down, keeping the rolls from touching one another. Making sure to place a plastic wrap in between each layer of spring rolls, continue until you have finished rolling 48 spring rolls.

Fill a shallow, medium pot such as a sauté pan halfway with oil over medium heat, and heat the oil to 360°F to 375°F. Working in small batches so as not to cool the oil too much, carefully lower a handful of spring rolls, making sure to separate them as the oil sizzles around them. Turning them occasionally, deep-fry until golden and crisp, 3 to 5 minutes. With a slotted spoon, transfer the spring rolls to a paper towel–lined cookie sheet.

Meanwhile, arrange the lettuce leaves, the remaining carrots, the cucumber, and mint leaves in individual piles. Divide the dipping sauce among four to six rice bowls. To eat, wrap a spring roll in a lettuce leaf and add a small amount of carrots, cucumber slices, and a mint leaf or two; then dip in the sauce.

# FRESH TOFU SUMMER ROLLS

*Serves 6; makes 24 rolls*

Summer rolls, or fresh spring rolls, are a wonderfully light alternative to deep-fried spring rolls. Filled with tofu, asparagus, and shredded lettuce, they are perfect for summer when hot temperatures warrant cooling foods (and hence the name). It is important to remove the ribs from the lettuce leaves so as not to tear through the delicate rice papers. Rice paper is extremely fragile, yet the rolls must hold together. This means that they have to be rolled tightly. Too loose and it will look unattractive. Too tight and it will break. Practice definitely makes perfect when making these fresh rolls.

1 tablespoon vegetable oil

1 pound firm tofu, cut into ½-inch-thick slices

1 small to medium head Boston lettuce, ribs removed, leaves cut into ½-inch strips

1 bunch asparagus, trimmed, steamed until tender, and cut into 2-inch-long pieces

1 large carrot, peeled and julienned into 2-inch-long pieces

48 fresh mint leaves, or 1 cup cilantro leaves

2 scallions, trimmed and julienned into 2-inch-long pieces

24 round rice papers (8 inches in diameter)

Asian Peanut Sauce (page 42)

Heat the oil in a nonstick skillet over medium heat, and pan-fry the tofu slices until golden and crisp on both sides, about 10 minutes total. Drain on a paper towel–lined plate, cool, and cut into strips 2 inches long and ½ inch thick, about the size of thick french-fries.

On a large platter, arrange the lettuce, asparagus, carrot, mint or cilantro leaves, scallions, and tofu sticks in individual piles, one next to the other.

Fill a rectangular baking pan halfway with lukewarm water. Arrange a lint-free kitchen towel on your work surface. Have a second lint-free kitchen towel for blotting. Soak 2 rice papers, one at a time, separating them as you add them to the water, until pliable and fully softened, about 3 minutes. Carefully lift and place them flat, one next to the other, on the towel. With the other towel blot them dry. (You want to work with a paper that is sticky, not wet and slippery.)

On the side closest to you and 1 inch from the edge, place a couple of pieces of tofu and asparagus, followed by small amounts of the lettuce, carrots, mint, and scallions. (Be light-handed here, as overstuffing your paper will probably result in tearing.) Lift up the edge of the paper closest to you and fold over the filling. Fold in the sides, and continue to roll to the end. (It should be tight, but not so tight that you tear it. You do not want a flabby-looking roll.) Repeat until you have 24 rolls. Serve with Asian Peanut Sauce on the side for dipping.

# VEGETABLE EGG ROLLS OR SPRING ROLLS

Serves 6; makes 18 egg rolls

Chinese egg rolls, known as *dan guen* in Cantonese, are made with thick egg roll wrappers, while spring rolls (*chun guen*) are made with paper-thin square or round wheat wrappers. Both are tasty wrapped around a filling of cabbage, bamboo shoot, and mushrooms. When rolled up, *dan guen* should be about 1½ inches in diameter, while the more delicate *chun guen*, only about 1 inch. Both should be about 3 inches long. The thin wheat spring roll wrappers and the thick egg roll wrappers can be found in Asian markets and in some health food stores.

¼  cup thin soy sauce

¼  cup rice vinegar

2  ounces fresh ginger, finely grated

2  tablespoons vegetable oil, plus more for deep-frying

1  large garlic clove, minced

1  small Napa cabbage, finely shredded

8  fresh shiitake mushrooms, stemmed, and caps finely chopped

1  large carrot, peeled and shredded

1  small bamboo shoot (about 1.5 ounces), finely chopped

1  teaspoon dark sesame oil

Freshly ground black pepper

18  thin wheat spring roll or thick egg roll wrappers

1  large egg, beaten

In a small bowl, mix together the soy sauce, vinegar, and ginger. Set the dipping sauce aside.

Heat the 2 tablespoons of oil in a skillet or wok over high heat, and stir-fry the garlic until fragrant, about 10 seconds. Add the cabbage, shiitakes, carrot, and bamboo shoot, and continue to stir-fry until the vegetables are cooked down and wilted, and all moisture has evaporated, about 13 minutes. (The stir-fry should be completely dry.) Set aside to cool, then toss with the sesame oil and pepper to taste.

Fill a medium pot halfway with oil and heat to to 360°F to 375°F.

Meanwhile make the egg or spring rolls. Place a wrapper in front of you so that one of the corners is close to you, and the wrapper looks like a diamond. Place about 2 tablespoons of vegetable filling 1 inch from the corner edge of the wrapper closest to you. Lift the edge of the wrapper closest to you and fold over the filling. Fold in the sides. Brush the rest of the wrapper lightly with the egg wash and continue to roll it up, sealing the filling. Set the roll, seam side down, on a cookie sheet lined with wax paper. Repeat with the remaing wrappers and filling for a total of 18 rolls.

Working in batches, so as not to cool the oil too much, deep-fry the rolls until golden and crisp on all sides, about 1 to 2 minutes per batch. Drain on a paper towel–lined plate and serve with the dipping sauce on the side.

# STEAMED BROAD RICE NOODLES STUFFED WITH FRESH SHRIMP

**Serves 6; makes 12 rolls**

Fresh broad rice noodles are versatile. They can be cut into strips and stir-fried or added to clear soups. The large sheets can also be cut into small squares and folded around all sorts of proteins, including shrimp. This dish is often served in dim sum restaurants, usually three per plate. The unseasoned fresh rice noodle rolls are steamed and served with soy sauce and chili sauce on the side for dipping. I like to serve the dish with a side of soy sauce, rich with stir-fried herbs and chilies. There is no substitute for the fresh broad rice noodles called for in this recipe, and they must be purchased fresh and used the same day, without being refrigerated.

¼  cup thin soy sauce

2  tablespoons vegetable oil

2  scallions, trimmed and julienned into thin 2-inch-long strips

2  red Thai chilies, seeded, stemmed, and thinly sliced into rounds

2  cups fresh cilantro leaves

1  pound fresh broad rice noodles, cut into 12 squares (about 3 inches each)

12  medium headless tiger shrimp, shelled, halved lengthwise, and deveined

Pour the soy sauce into a medium heat-proof bowl.

Meanwhile, in a saucepan, heat the oil over high heat. Stir-fry the scallions and chilies until wilted and pale gold, about 3 minutes. Add the cilantro and continue to stir-fry until wilted, about 2 minutes. Transfer everything, including the fragrant oil, to the soy sauce. Let stand until ready to serve.

Take a rice noodle square and place 3 shrimp halves in line with one edge, fold over to enclose the shrimp, and fold over again. You should have a 1 x 3-inch rectangle. Repeat the process 11 more times, and place the rolls on heat-proof plates.

Place a wok filled halfway with water over high heat. Place a plate filled with rice noodle rolls on each tier of a bamboo steamer. Put the steamer over the wok and place the lid on top. Steam until the shrimp is cooked through and becomes opaque, about 5 minutes.

Put 2 steamed rolls on each small plate. Serve with the herbal soy sauce on the side, and instruct guests to drizzle the sauce over their shrimp rolls.

# MAIL-ORDER SOURCES

Although the majority of the ingredients needed for the recipes in this book are readily available, I have listed below a few reputable sources, which you can visit online. At the touch of a button, they'll be happy to ship ingredients such as curry paste, tamarind, noodles, and dried shrimp directly to your home, along with cooking equipment in some cases.

### Diamond Organics
Highway 1
Moss Landing, CA 95039
Tel: (888) ORGANIC (674-2642)
E-mail: info@diamondorganics.com
Web site: www.diamondorganics.com
*Asian herbs and vegetables*

### Importfood.com
P.O. Box 2054
Issaquah, WA 98027
Tel: (888) 618-THAI (8424)
E-mail: info@importfood.com
Web site: www.importfood.com
*Southeast Asian condiments and dried ingredients*

### Kalustyan's
c/o Marhaha International, Inc.
123 Lexington Avenue
New York, NY 10016
Tel: (800) 352-3451
E-mail: sales@kalustyans.com
Web site: www.kalustyans.com
*Dried spices*

### KA-ME Foods
Web site: www.kame.com
*Readily available all-natural Asian noodles and condiments.*

### Melissa's World Variety Produce, Inc.
P.O. Box 21127
Los Angeles, CA 90021
Tel: (800) 588-0151
E-mail: hotline@melissas.com
Web site: www.melissas.com
*Asian herbs and vegetables*

### Mitsuwa Marketplace
595 River Road
Edgewater, NJ 07020
Tel: (201) 941-9113
E-mail: newjersey@mitsuwa.com
Web site: www.mitsuwanj.com
*Japanese and Korean ingredients*

### Pearl River
477 Broadway
New York, NY 10013
Tel: (800) 878-2446
E-mail: pearlriver@pearlriver.com
Web site: www.pearlriver.com
*Asian cooking equipment and dried ingredients*

### Penzeys Spices
Tel: (800) 741-7787
Call for store locations
Web site: www.penzeys.com
*Dried spices*

# INDEX

# TABLE OF EQUIVALENTS

The exact equivalents in the following tables have been rounded for convenience.

### LIQUID/DRY MEASURES

| U.S. | Metric |
|---|---|
| ¼ teaspoon | 1.25 milliliters |
| ½ teaspoon | 2.5 milliliters |
| 1 teaspoon | 5 milliliters |
| 1 tablespoon (3 teaspoons) | 15 milliliters |
| 1 fluid ounce (2 tablespoons) | 30 milliliters |
| ¼ cup | 60 milliliters |
| ⅓ cup | 80 milliliters |
| ½ cup | 120 milliliters |
| 1 cup | 240 milliliters |
| 1 pint (2 cups) | 480 milliliters |
| 1 quart (4 cups, 32 ounces) | 960 milliliters |
| 1 gallon (4 quarts) | 3.84 liters |
| 1 ounce (by weight) | 28 grams |
| 1 pound | 448 grams |
| 2.2 pounds | 1 kilogram |

### OVEN TEMPERATURE

| Fahrenheit | Celsius | Gas |
|---|---|---|
| 250 | 120 | ½ |
| 275 | 140 | 1 |
| 300 | 150 | 2 |
| 325 | 160 | 3 |
| 350 | 180 | 4 |
| 375 | 190 | 5 |
| 400 | 200 | 6 |
| 425 | 220 | 7 |
| 450 | 230 | 8 |
| 475 | 240 | 9 |
| 500 | 260 | 10 |

### LENGTH

| U.S. | Metric |
|---|---|
| ⅛ inch | 3 millimeters |
| ¼ inch | 6 millimeters |
| ½ inch | 12 millimeters |
| 1 inch | 2.5 centimeters |